OVERCOMING

CHURCH

HURT

You can serve God again

JEFF GRACER

Dedication

I dedicate this book to my dear mother Verinas, my two sisters Jessy and Madaliso.I also devote this book to the Grace for Grace Ministries. You are amazing people and I know that you can overcome church hurt and serve God again.

I wish to further commit this book to all who have left church, those who are inactive in church and have decided to retreat themselves to home dwelling. The good news is that you can all overcome church hurt and serve God gain.

Acknowledgements

I want to first of all acknowledge my Lord and Savior, Jesus Christ; the owner, builder and groom of the church. Dear Lord, I am grateful for the privilege to serve in your house.

I am also grateful to God for my friends and fellow ministers who were there to encourage me through the writing period.

Endorsements

"'Hurting people will always hurt others.' The Bible says 'whose feet they HURT, he was laid in iron…' (Psalm 105:18). Apostle Jeff has taken his time to do an X-ray of the hidden truths that have made many very vulnerable in their service to God. From dealing with falsehood to enslavement to moral failure and many other vices; Apostle Jeff has exposed the reality of the big elephant in the room.Don't just read this, study it. I recommend it in strong terms"- Apostle Professor Johnson Suleman.

In this present world there are so many forces trying so hard to stop believers from fulfilling their God given destiny. Through the words contained in this book, I believe many will find comfort, strength, healing and love. My son in the faith, Apostle Jeff Gracer; has perfectly handled, one of the sensitive and timely message in Christendom which alot of ministries are struggling with today.

This is the subject which has touched many, yet many could not overcome it, as a result they ended up making wrong decisions which costed their destinies. I can describe this book as God's medicine to the hurting believers and unbelievers out there. I encourage you to meditatively read this book and walk through the process of healing and serve God again.

God heals and restores. This book is pointing the victims of church hurt to the place of healing as well as offering an encouragement that we are troubled on every side, yet not distressed; we are perplexed, but not in despair; Persecuted, but not forsaken; cast down, but not destroyed; Always bearing about in the body the dying of the Lord Jesus, that the life also of Jesus might be made manifest in our body.

Today the kingdom of God has come in your life, for this is the day of your healing.

Apostle DR. Sunday Sinyangwe.

We live in a time when many people look up to the church as a place of healing. However, many people flock to the church when they have already encountered a traumatic experience in their lives. Since many typical Christian Zambians don't really seek counseling when they are hurt or have a mental health challenge in life, such people usually end up hurting other people knowingly or unknowingly within the Christian environments.

This book is bringing the necessary awareness of how the church can hurt its own members and how such traumatic encounters can lead to major mental health impairment in one's life. Apostle Jeff, has dived into broader issues which Christian culture has hidden for long and I believe, the revelations shared through this book will bring healing to many children of God.

Paul Dimitroth

Clinical psychologist

In a day and age when many believers are turning away from the church on account of "lawlessness", Overcoming Church Hurt is a breath of fresh air as the author attempts to tackle head-on the factors behind this scourge, why it happens, how it happens and best of all, how to overcome as a victim and still maintain the fervency and zeal for God - something that many do not manage.

Rev Walter Mwambazi - Author - "Five Major Reasons Africa is Poor

Disclaimer

This book is not a book for newly converted Christians who are just getting to know the Lord or just starting out in their Christian journey. If you are a new convert, this may not be the right book for you at this point. This book is for people who have been Christians for some time and have gone through issues you may not understand until you pass through a similar situation.

If you are just start starting out in your Christian journey, please drop this book now and visit the nearest Christian book store and ask them to direct you to other books that will help you build a strong foundation in your Christian journey.

This book is for people who have gone through painful issues in church and carry scars they received from within the house of God.

If you are in this category, this book will help you get to a place of healing and shall encourage you to continue your fight of faith. But if you are not, please stop reading this book now! You will not understand the issues and topics discussed in this book. You are vulnerable to criticize what you don't fully understand.

OVERCOMING CHURCH HURT

By Jeff Gracer

An Overview

Have you been hurt in church before? Are you somebody still grappling with hurts from what was done to you in church? Or are you related or acquainted with somebody who has been hurt from church? Whatever position you are at, **Overcoming Church Hurt** is just the book you need.

In this book the author aims to bring to light the reality of church hurt; what causes it, who is behind it, and at what cost it affects the people in church and society. He also discusses mental health in relation with church hurt paying attention to mental issues. Further, practical steps based on the Holy Scriptures for bringing victory and healing are discussed with the intent to help victims recover fully and serve God again.

There are many people in church who are hurting silently and many more have left the church and given up on the faith altogether. Some have gone back to the world. We can neither ignore nor pretend about what happened to them.

The author therefore establishes from the onset, the fact that if one is a victim of church hurt, he or she must know that church hurt is nothing new but has been there and was there even in the early church as revealed in the records of church history from biblical times down to the recent past. Moreover, hurt is real in today's church.

Church hurt is a result of many factors. It is caused by falsehood in the church, how the clergy negatively handle people from the pulpit and through their compromised discharge of spiritual duties, religious enslavement advanced through legalism, manipulation, exploitation and abuse of people and moral failure in the church, especially that which is exhibited by those in positions of authority. Furthermore, church hurt has by and large been found to be related to mental illnesses and mental disorders in the church. Sometimes people come to church come with mental illnesses and disorders. In some cases, church hurt is responsible for triggering mental illnesses among the people in church or may make mental illness cases worse. Some people come to church, get hurt perhaps through gossip, abuse, exploitation or any other way and become mentally ill with conditions such as depression and suicidal thoughts among other things.

It has become common to hear of depression cases and suicide cases right from faithful church goers. In this book, the author discusses how the church can play an important role in one's mental health care.

Church hurt comes at a great cost. Once hurt in church, many abandon the faith and lose zeal for the work of God. Church hurt breaks great ministry partnerships and causes shame and ridicule on the church. Church hurt also hardens the hearts of non-believers, making them to lose interest in anything to do with religion. It contributes to the stagnation of churches and brings depression and discouragement among many believers. This book discusses confusion as the fundamental source of church hurt.

It is imperative that the reader understands the church society. The author is of the view that the church has people at three levels: the near perfect without spot or wrinkle, the mixed multitude and a group of those who may have abandoned the faith already but still come to church. Having such a combination of people in the church make church hurt an obvious occurrence.

At the height of the book, the author inspires and compels the reader to learn and follow practical but spiritual steps to overcome church hurt, and he brings the book to a conclusion by giving out further steps to receiving healing from church hurt and become the better person that would rise from it and serve God again.

Table of Contents

Introduction

- CHAPTER 1: The Reality of Church Hurt

- CHAPTER 2: Church Hurt in the Early Church

- CHAPTER 3: Church Hurt in Today's Church

- CHAPTER 4: Who is Behind Church Hurt

- CHAPTER 5: The Cost of Church Hurt

- CHAPTER 6: Falsehood in the Church

- CHAPTER 7: Hurt from the Pulpit

- CHAPTER 8: Religious Enslavement

- CHAPTER 9: Moral Failure

- CHAPTER 10: Understanding the Church Society

- CHAPTER 11: Church Hurt and Mental Health

- CHAPTER 12: Church Hurt and the Homosexual Community

- CHAPTER 13: Steps to Overcoming Church Hurt

- CHAPTER 14: Receiving Healing from Church Hurt

- CHAPTER 15: You can Serve God Again

Conclusion

A Prayer

Church hurt has been a silent but one of the most-deadly strategies the enemy has used over the years to destabilize believers, subvert people's callings and separate great ministry partnerships. Church hurt has contributed to low church attendance, contributed to the increase of depression and other mental illnesses in religious circles. **Overcoming Church Hurt** was written out of the author's burden and desire to see people who have stopped serving God in church due to various hurtful occasions recover and fully resume their responsibility in the house of God.

It is also written from various observations, numerous scriptural references, research and experiences in dealing with people that have been hurt in church.

Church hurt is real and people get hurt in church from the pulpit through the false teachings and fake prophecies that they may encounter. Church hurt also sprouts from the moral failures especially among church leaders. It can also emerge from unfortunate tragedies and accidents that happen under the church jurisdiction. There are several other causes of hurt within the church.

Church hurt is a matter that is often overlooked. We have a church that is full of hurting people. Most people come to church to find healing as they should, but unfortunately, they find an imperfect church full of people equally hurting like themselves. I have seen ushers hurt people walking into church. I have seen people who are supposed to be hospitable to new people in church turning out to be hurtful to them. I have seen preachers hurt people from their insensitive sermons, false teachings and practices from the pulpit. I have seen people get hurt by gossip in church.I have seen immoral behavior and lifestyle by church leaders hurting people in church.I have seen pastors getting hurt by members of their churches. I have seen how some people have gotten hurt after tragedies that have happened right in church or on church mission trips. There is a lot of hurt that individuals experience surrounding the church. Pretending that the hurt people go through from within the church is not serious will not help anybody. We must all be awake to this reality today and try to find the remedy for the hurting. We must be alive to the truths that can heal and set us free.

Join me as we journey through overcoming church hurt step by step. This book will help you understand the church society, compel you to arise above church hurt and help you to see the possibility of living free from church hurt and find personal healing. With God all things are possible.

CHAPTER 1

THE REALITY OF CHURCH HURT

"Then He said to the disciples, 'It is impossible that no offenses should come, but woe to him through whom they come! It would be better for him if a millstone were hung around his neck, and he were thrown into the sea, than that he should offend one of these little ones. Take heed to yourselves. If your brother sins against you, rebuke him; and if he repents forgive him. And if he sins against you seven times in a day, and seven times in a day returns to you, saying, I repent,' you

Like any other society where there are people, even in the church, there will be misunderstandings. Believers will hurt one another, pastors will hurt their flock, leaders will hurt church members and this unfortunately is inevitable.

Our Lord Jesus made us aware of this fact in Mathew 18:15-17 and he said,

"If a fellow believer hurts you, go and tell him — work it out between the two of you. If he listens, you've made a friend. If he won't listen, take one or two others along so that the presence of witnesses will keep things honest, and try again. If he still won't listen, tell the church. If he won't listen to the church, you'll have to start over from scratch, confront him with the need for repentance, and offer again God's forgiving love" (Matt 18:15-17 Paraphrased).

This verse highlights to us the possibility of being hurt by a fellow believer and the procedure for reconciliation. But my interest is in the brother who rejects to reconcile despite the attempts to make peace. Sometimes you can be so hurt that no matter how much people try to come in and intervene, all their efforts become futile. Church hurt can be so painful that only God will heal and restore certain relationships. There are people who will not easily recover from church hurt because they have been so hurt that they ignore the instruction of the Word of God to forgive. It is honestly not easy to forgive in church. But I believe after you are done reading this book, you will be greatly helped by the Holy Spirit to overcome church hurt and you will be victorious over the secret pains you got from church.

My Church Background

Growing up in as a young boy in Livingstone, Zambia, I grew up seeing my dear mother as a very committed Christian and regular church attendee. She attended every single service. As a matter of fact, I remember seeing her waking up as early as 06:00hrs in the morning and heading to the church building with her friends and they would always clean the church building and prepare the place for the service which was to start at 09:00hrs. So, imagine how involved we were in church affairs. My family was a hundred percent engaged in practically everything in church. Though she was not the lead pastor, I observed that my mother would always remain behind and sort out issues among other church members as she was entrusted.

A few years later, I wondered why mom stopped going to church, she was no longer waking up early in the morning to go and clean up the church building as per routine. She didn't stop us from going to church but rather remained at home. I also discovered that her friends had also stopped going to church and had moved to another church. We then relocated from the house we were living in and moved to another further location away from the church and we could not manage to walk all the way down to church. We then split churches. My mom and my elder sister joined a church close by our new residence. Myself and my younger sister joined a church that had just opened a little further from our house but the distance was manageable to walk, just about forty-minute walk.

All I knew growing up was church life, but by the time we shifted from the first church to the second, I was at my teenage phase. That's the time you want to taste the things of the world. I remember I was in my ninth grade when all this was happening. I had lost touch with church for about three to five months and went wild. But by the grace of God before I went too far into the world, Jesus came and saved me.

By the time I got to high school, I had gotten my church life back on track and joined the choir where I played the keyboard and guitar for the new church. Now, at the new church, I would still hear issues in the background. People would join the church and after a while leave the church. I would wonder what was wrong but there would always be one issue or another. Even the one you thought was very committed and loyal would one day get to a point where they leave and join another church, you would also hear that they have also moved to another church for some undisclosed reason. The bottom line is that they were hurt by someone in one way or another. It is either they were hurt by someone in the church or by the pastor.

Church Hurt Is Real

To deny the reality of church hurt is a grave mistake. Being a pastor for over a decade, I have acknowledged the reality of church hurt. In today's church, many people have to endure to stay in church. Many have come to struggle to stay happy in church. The church community has become a hostile environment for many, unfortunately. A place that was supposed to be a happy place has become a hostile place. A place that was supposed to be a place of prayer has become a place of pain. An encouragement center has rather discouraged many people.

Today, you have to think twice before you join a church. People today join new churches with defensive mechanisms because of the hurt they have experienced from previous churches. Others have seen their family or close relatives go through terrible hurt whilst in church and have vowed never to associate themselves to the church in fear of church hurt. With the introduction of the online streaming of services, it seems to be a prayer answered to many who are connected to a particular man or woman of God as they would simply watch the church services online and avoid physical gathering for the fear of being hurt when they physically mingle with people in church.

My interactions with non-gospel musicians have made me realize that church hurt has its influence in why these talented people don't sing gospel. These people are greatly talented in genres or types of music which are not popular in church. Some have revealed that the main reason they don't sing gospel or go to church anymore is because they were hurt by the rejection which they received from the church folk.

A newly born again professional fashion model once told me that she stopped going to church because people would look at her in an awkward manner because her social media accounts contained her half naked pictures, so rather went back to the world where she is accepted and not condemned. You may say, she has to delete every half naked picture on her platforms since she is now born again. Absolutely so, but you are forgetting that God works on people's transformation at different levels.

When children grow up seeing their mothers and fathers crying, weeping as a result of church issues, it makes their hearts become resentful and resistant towards anything that has to do with the church. The church plays an important role in the development of society. It is from church that good morals are taught. This is in sight of a society whose families are becoming more dysfunctional. Parents today are not available to train up children in the way of the Lord so that when they grow up, they may maintain the ways of purity. Most parents are busy pursuing different things at the expense of training their children in the way of the Lord. We also have a lot of single headed families due to the high rate of divorce and pregnancies outside marriage.

Children who grow up by themselves usually don't get to know what is right or wrong. The church is supposed to come in and train such children into becoming responsible young men and women.

However, sometimes when they go to church, they find the environment is hurtful, resentful, hostile and unfriendly causing them to go to the wrong places and other religions which gladly receive them with open arms.

What makes church hurt so painful is the fact that church is where most of us learn the love of our heavenly Father from. The love of God is taught at church. We learn from church about how much God loves us and how Christ gave up His life for us. As we begin to attend church, we are so much in love with Christ and our hearts are so open to receive from the Lord. Church is the place we connect in worship and prayer at a deeper level as compared to when we are elsewhere. We are so excited to belong to a new spiritual family in Christ and everything feels perfect. Then suddenly we get hurt by the same people we call brothers and sisters. Someone once said to me "I have been more hurt in church more than anywhere else." That's a sad reality.

CHAPTER 2

CHURCH HURT IN THE EARLY CHURCH

"Now in those days, when the number of the disciples was multiplying, there arose a complaint against the Hebrews by the Hellenists, because their widows were neglected in the daily distribution" (Acts 6:1)

The Hellenists Widows' Complaint

As the early church was growing in the number of disciples, so were the problems among the brethren. In those days in Jerusalem, the church had a social welfare ministry to widows. Widows who had nobody to take care of them were supplied with aid from the church. Every day there used to be distribution of food and basic material supplies. However, complaints arose against the Hebrews (native Jews) by the Hellenists (Greek-speaking Jews), because their widows were neglected in the daily welfare distributions.

The Hellenists were hurt by the prejudice and selective actions of the Hebrews in the way they handled the widows' daily distribution. They felt their Hebrew counterparts were acting unfairly toward their widows, and they raised a complaint against them.The church was going through some growing pains of trying to keep up with everyone in the midst of rapid growth and had neglected, most probably without intent, the widows among the Hellenists (believersestudy: 2020)

"Now in those days, when the number of disciples was multiplying, there arose a complaint against the Hebrews by the Hellenists, because their

widows were neglected in the daily distribution"
(Acts 6:1)

This was a mixed church. It was a church with native Jewish members and also with Greek-speaking Jewish members. Therefore, it was a church with a cultural mix. Now, the native Jews seemed to have an attitude of superiority over their counterparts. They felt they had a bigger stake in the church. They thought their fellow native Jewish widows deserved larger portions and preferential treatment in the daily distributionthan the Greek-speaking Jewish widows. You must know that Salvation is from the Jews, and that the Jews were the first to be in covenant with God and to receive the Law and the commandments. This status made them feel like they were the bona-fide people of God as opposed to anybody else, including those they felt did not culturally live like them.

The selective actions of the native Jews brought hurt on the Greek-speaking Jews and this not only revealed the underlying negative perceptions and attitudes that they had against their counterparts, but also became a threat to the unity of the church. This divisive dispute came to the attention of the apostles. The apostles intervened accordingly by creating a strategic leadership intervention. When people feel neglected, treated unfairly and prejudiced against in the church, it brings hurt on them and disturbs the peace, unity and progress of the church.

The apostles instructed the church to choose men from among themselves; men with a good reputation, full of the Holy Spirit and wisdom, to be in charge of the said social welfare ministry of widows' daily distribution. This decision pleased the whole church. The people selected a mix of both native Jewish deacons and Greek-speaking Jewish deacons, and that brought balance, fairness and unity among them. This stability made the preaching of the gospel spread and the number of disciples multiplied greatly across the whole city of Jerusalem, and many priests became believers.

"Then the twelve summoned the multitude of disciples and said, 'It is not desirable that we should leave the word of God and serve tables. Therefore, brethren, seek out from among you seven men of good reputation, full of the Holy Spirit and wisdom, whom we may appoint over this business, but we will give ourselves continually to prayer and to the ministry of the word. And the saying pleased the whole multitude. And they

chose Stephen, a man full of faith and the Holy Spirit, and Philip, Prochorus, Nicanor, Timon, Parmenas and Nicolas, a proselyte from Antioch, whom they set before the apostles; and when they had prayed, they laid hands on them. Then the word of God spread, and the number of disciples multiplied greatly in Jerusalem, and a great many of the priests were obedient to the faith" (Acts 6:2-7)

This wise and firm leadership decision from the apostles settled the church hurt the widows were feeling and there was peace, unity and progress in the church.

The Jewish Christians' Contention against Peter

Though some Jewish people had become believers in Christ, there was still a lot of work to be done in terms of mindset change among them. Most Jews had the perception and belief that God was just the God of the Jews only, and that salvation was theirs and should never be shared with any other nation and people. Culturally, they did not want to mix with the Gentiles (nations), and for most, even upon their salvation in Christ, they still held on to that perception and belief.

When the Jewish believers in Judea heard that the apostle Peter had gone to the Gentiles and had eaten with them and preached the gospel to them, they were hurt and as such contended against him. But Peter narrated to them the divine encounter he had that changed his perception and belief toward the Gentiles and how he heard the voice of the Lord instructing him to go and preach to them. He further gave them enough evidence of how he could not resist the Lord but obey Him, and how the Gentiles too were given the same gift of the Holy Spirit with the evidence of speaking in tongues. Then every mouth was shut and all glorified God, realizing that God had granted the Gentiles repentance to real life just like them.

"Then he said to them, 'You know how unlawful it is for a Jewish man to keep company with or go to one of another nation. But God has shown me that I should not call any man common or unclean. Therefore, I came without objection as soon as I was sent for. I ask, then, for what reason have you sent for me?... Then Peter opened his mouth and said: 'In truth I perceive that God shows no partiality. But in every nation whoever fears Him and works righteousness is accepted by Him...' While Peter was speaking these words, the Holy

Spirit fell upon all those who heard the word. And those of the circumcision who believed were astonished, as many as came with Peter, because the gift of the Holy Spirit had been poured out on the Gentiles also. For they heard them speak with tongues and magnify God" (Acts 10:28,29,34,35,44-46)

"Now the apostles and brethren who were in Judea heard that the Gentiles had also received the word of God. And when Peter came to Jerusalem, those of the circumcision contended with him, saying, 'You went in to uncircumcised men and ate with them!' But Peter explained it to them in order from the beginning... When they heard these things, they became silent; and they glorified God, saying, 'Then has God granted to the Gentiles repentance to life" (Acts 11:1-4,18)

You would think when Peter's fellow Jewish believers at Jerusalem heard that he had gone to preach the gospel to the Gentiles and that the Gentiles had also become believers and received the Holy Spirit would be happy, but no! They got hurt and prepared for a very hostile meeting with Peter to confront him for his "compromise."

There are people in the church that are so religious that they separate from others on cultural or religious grounds, with a 'holier than thou" attitude and behavior. Strangely, they get hurt when they see one who doesn't seem to hold their prejudiced perceptions and beliefs. Such people want other people in the church to behave like them, talk like them, dress like them, and generally do things like them. These are a kind of the people that spread negative energy in the church. Such people are hostile, they contend and hurt others whom they perceive not to be adhering to their negative beliefs and opinions.

The Sharp Disagreement between Barnabas and Paul

Barnabas and Paul had been great ministry partners for a considerably good period. In fact, their partnership was authored by the Holy Spirit of God. Before his conversion to the Christian faith, Paul who was then called Saul persecuted the church. However, on his way to Damascus with authority to arrest believers, he had an encounter with Jesus, and through that encounter he became a believer. At first the believers were hesitant to trust him but as he grew in strength in the knowledge of the Lord and in ministry, more trusted him, and when the unbelieving Jews wanted to kill him, Barnabas, who had a testimony of being a good man, full of the Holy Spirit and of faith, took him and brought him to Antioch and the two formed a great ministry partnership, teaching the believers at Antioch for some time. It was while they were at Antioch fasting and praying together with others that the Holy Spirit spoke concerningBarnabas and Paul, commissioning them as Apostles.

"But some of them were men from Cyprus and Cyrene, who, when they had come to Antioch, spoke to the Hellenists, preaching the Lord Jesus. And the hand of the Lord was with them, and a great number believed and turned to the Lord. Then news of these things came to the ears of the ears of the church in Jerusalem, and they sent Barnabas to go as far as Antioch. When he came and had seen the grace of God, he was glad, and encouraged them all that with purpose of heart they should continue with the Lord. For he was a good man, full of the Holy Spirit and of faith. And a great many people were added to the Lord. Then Barnabas departed for Tarsus to seek Saul. And when he had found him, he brought him to Antioch. So it was that for the whole year they

*assembled with the church and taught a great
many people. And the disciples were first called
Christians in Antioch"*

(Acts 11:20-26)

*"Now in the church that was at Antioch there were
certain prophets and teachers: Barnabas, Simeon
who was called Niger, Lucius of Cyrene, Manaen
who had been brought up with Herod the Tetrarch,
and Saul. As ministered to the Lord and fasted, the
Holy Spirit said, 'Now separate to Me Barnabas
and Saul for the work to which I have called them.'
Then, having fasted and prayed, and laid hands on
them, they sent them away"*

(Acts 13:1-3)

However, what was a Holy Spirit birthed apostolic
ministry partnership between these two men was
broken when they had a sharp disagreement about
their assistant John Mark. John was a young man
whom they had taken from Jerusalem into their
team but when persecution arose and the mission
became difficult, he abandoned them in the
mission field. When time to go on their second
missionary journey, Barnabas wanted John to join
them, but Paul disagreed, and their disagreement
was only resolved by separation and that was the

end of the once strong and mighty apostolic ministry partnership.

"And Barnabas and Saul returned from Jerusalem when they had fulfilled their ministry, and they also took with them John whose surname was Mark"

(Acts 12:25)

"Then after some days Paul said to Barnabas, 'Let us now go back and visit our brethren in every city where we have preached the word of the Lord, and see how they are doing.' Now Barnabas was determined to take with them John called Mark, but Paul insisted that they should not take with them the one who had departed from them in Pamphylia, and had not gone with them to the work. Then the contention became so sharp that they parted from one another. And so Barnabas took Mark and sailed to Cyprus; but Paul chose Silas and departed, being commended by the brethren to the grace of God. And he went through Syria and Cilicia, strengthening the churches"

(Acts 36-41)

Clearly, Paul had been hurt by John Mark's action of having abandoned them in the heat of persecution and difficulty on the mission field, and when Barnabas determined to take the young man on the field again, it aroused the hurt in Paul again and Paul would not have them take him along with them. Their conversation went from bad to worse, as they disagreed sharply about it and even parted ways. They parted ways on account of somebody. John Mark became the reason for their hurts and the end of their partnership. Barnabas took John Mark with him and sailed to Cyprus, while Paul took Silas and went through Syria and Cilicia, strengthening the brethren.

Beware that you don't destroy partnerships the Holy Spirit has joined together. May you not be responsible for church hurt and separation among great ministry partners and may you not weaken or cause the breaking down of the team.

It appears Barnabas was for John Mark while Paul preferred Silas, and the end was division and breakdown of their partnership. From that point on we never get to hear about Barnabas.Overtime, John Mark had matured in ministry and proven himself to be useful and dependable that Paul, having forgiven him, requested for him and his services.

"Only Luke is with me. Get Mark and bring him with you, for he is useful to me for ministry" (2 Tim 4:11)

The Separatist Attitude of Peter, Barnabas and the Jewish believers towards the Gentile Believers

You would think, Peter, having been the first apostle and Jewish believer to whom God revealed Himself in an extraordinary way to change his perception and belief about Gentiles. Peter had gone to eat with them and even preach to them, and had given report to his fellow Jewish believers that the Gentiles were just like them in the faith, would never behave with prejudice toward Gentiles ever again. But the reality is that perceptions and beliefs die hard.

When Peter went to visit the Church at Antioch, a church mixed with both Gentiles and Jews, peter acted hypocritically. Before certain Jewish believers joined him from Jerusalem, he would eat with the Gentile believers but when they came, he withdrew and separated himself and would not eat nor interact with them. He only interacted with the Jewish believers. Peter's influence also affected Barnabas and the rest of the team. His actions together with Barnabas and the rest of the group of Jews obviously hurt their Gentile counterparts. Paul noticed this hypocritical attitude and had to call Peter to order.

"But when Peter came to Antioch, I had to oppose him to his face, for what he did was very wrong. When he first arrived, he ate with the Gentile believers who were not circumcised, but afterward, when some friends of James came, Peter wouldn't eat with the Gentiles anymore. He was afraid of criticism from these people who insisted on the necessity of circumcision. As a result, other Jewish believers followed Peter's hypocrisy, and even Barnabas was led astray by their hypocrisy. When I saw that they were not following the truth of the gospel message, I said to Peter in front of all the others, 'Since you a Jew by birth have discarded the Jewish laws and are living like a Gentile, why are you now trying to make these Gentiles follow the Jewish traditions?"

(Gal 2:11-14)

Divisions in the Church

Before His betrayal, suffering and death on the cross, Jesus prayed for his disciples and all those who would believe in Him through their ministry that they may be one. The unity of the church was one of the paramount prayers for Jesus. His prayer was that unity will make the world to believe that God sent Him into the world. The unity of the church reveals the glory and character of God, because God is One (Father, Son and Holy Spirit).

"I am praying not only for these disciples but also for all who will ever believe in me through their message. I pray that they will be one, just as You and I are one – as You are in Me, Father and I am in You. and may they be in Us so that the world will believe You sent Me. I have given them the you gave Me, so they may be one as We are one. I am in them and You in Me. May they experience such perfect unity that the world will know that You sent Me and that You love them as much as You love Me"

(John 17:20-23, NLT0

"Hear, O Israel: The Lord our God, the Lord is one! You shall love the Lord your God with all your heart, with all your soul, and with all your strength"

(Deut 6:4-5)

Nevertheless, there were divisions in the early church. There was strife, envy and division, and that revealed the immaturity of believers in the church. With that in mind it is apparent that many people were being hurt in the church. Paul warned the believers in Rome of those who cause division and offenses, and instructed them to avoid such people. He could not have warned them if there was no possibility of having divisive and hurtful people among them. Paul also heard reports that there were contentions and divisions going on in the church at Corinth. The church was divided on grounds of the preachers and leaders each one favored and liked.

"Now I urge you, brethren, note those who cause divisions and offenses, contrary to the doctrine which you learned, and avoid them. For those who are such do not serve our Lord Jesus Christ, but their own belly, and by smooth words and flattering speech deceive the hearts of the simple"

(Rom 16:17-18)

"Now I plead with you, brethren, by the name of our Lord Jesus Christ, that you all speak the same thing and that there be no divisions among you, but that you be perfectly joined together in the

*same mind and in the same judgment. For it has
been declared to me concerning you, my brethren,
by those of Chloe's household, that each of you
says, "I am of Paul," or "I am of Apollos," or "I
am of Cephas," or "I am of Christ." Is Christ
divided? Was Paul crucified to for you? Or were
you baptized in the name of Paul?"*

(1 Cor 1:10-13)

*"And I, brethren, could not speak to you as to
spiritual people but as to carnal, as to babes in
Christ. I fed you with milk and with solid food; for
until now you were not able to receive it, and even
now you are still not able; for you are still carnal.
For where there are envy, strife and divisions
among you, are you not carnal and behaving like
mere men? For when one says, "I am of Paul,"
and another, "I am of Apollos," are you not
carnal. Who then is Paul, and who is Apollos, but
ministers through whom you believed, as the Lord
gave to each one?... Therefore, let no one boast in
men. For all things are yours; whether Paul or
Apollos or Cephas, or the world or life or death, or
things present or things to come – all are yours.
And you are Christ's, and Christ is God's"*

(1 Cor 3:1-5,21-23)

Gossipers in the Church

Gossip has been one of the most painful behaviors responsible for church hurt in the early church. Gossip is very hurtful and destructive. If you want to end church hurt, take out strife and contentions. If you want to end strife and contentions in the church, take out gossip.

"Seldom set foot in your neighbor's house, lest he become weary of you and hate you. A man who bears false witness against his neighbor is like a club, a sword, and a sharp arrow"

(Prov 25:17-18)

"Where there is no wood, the fire goes out; and where there is no talebearer, strife ceases. As charcoal is to burning coals, and wood to fire, so is a contentious man to kindle strife. The words of a talebearer are like tasty trifles, and they go down into the inmost body. Fervent lips with a wicked heart are like earthenware covered with silver dross"

(Prov 26:20-23)

Paul wrote a letter to warn the church at Thessalonica about lazy gossipers that were not working at all but were just busybodies, going from house to house spreading gossip, and he instructed the church to mark them, avoid them and keep no company with them, so that they may be ashamed, if perhaps that could make them to change their behavior. Their gossip obviously hurt people in the church.

"Yet we hear that some of you are living idle lives, refusing to work and meddling in other people's business. We command such people and urge them in the name of the Lord Jesus Christ to settle down and work to earn their own living. As for the rest of you, dear brothers and sisters, never get tired of doing good. Take note of those who refuse to obey what we say in this letter. Stay away from them so they will be ashamed. Don't think of them as enemies, but warn them as you would a brother or sister"

(2 Thes 3:11-15)

Paul received a report from those belonging to the family of Chloe about the divisions that were going on in the church at Corinth and he mentioned it to the church that the report came from those of the family of Chloe. If we must end gossip in church we must speak like Paul.

Falsehood in the Church at Crete

The early church experienced falsehood in great extents. In the church at Crete, there were false ministers and prophets who brought a lot of hurt and mental distress amongbelievers with their false teachings.

"For there are many disorderly and unruly men who are idle (vain, empty) and misleading talkers and self-deceivers and deceivers of others. This is true especially of those of the circumcision party (who come from Judaism). Their mouths must be stopped, for they are mentally distressing and subverting whole families by teaching what they ought not to teach, for the purpose of getting base advantage and disreputable gain. One of their very number, a prophet of their own, said, Cretans are always liars, hurtful beasts, idle and lazy gluttons, and this account of them is really true. Because it is true, rebuke them sharply (deal sternly, even severely with them), so that they may be sound in the faith and free from error" (Titus 1:10-13 Amplified)

CHAPTER **3**

CHURCH HURT IN TODAY'S CHURCH

"You should know this, Timothy, that in the last days there will be very difficult times. For people will love only themselves and their money. They will be boastful and proud, scoffing at God, disobedient to parents, and ungrateful. They will consider nothing sacred. They will be unloving and unforgiving; they will slander others and have no self-control. They will be cruel and hate what is good. They will betray their friends, be reckless, be puffed up with pride, and love pleasure rather than God. They will act religious, but they will reject the power that could make them godly. Stay away from people like that! They are the kind who work their way into people's homes and win the confidence of vulnerable women who are burdened with the guilt of sin and controlled by various

desires. Such women are forever following new teachings, but they are never able to understand the truth"

(2 Tim 3:1-7 NLT)

Genuine Love

We are living in the last days. The prophetic utterances of Paul are becoming more and more real today. The church is among the key places where some of the prophecies are finding their fulfilment. We have unloving, uncaring, unforgiving, ungrateful, selfish, rebellious, boastful, proud, treacherous, slandering, gossiping, hateful, cruel, covetous, pleasure lovers rather than God-lovers, money lovers, religious but ungodly people, vulnerable but seductive women that are ever acting religious but have no spiritual encounter and no knowledge of Jesus Christ, and false teachers and ministers in the church today. Beloved, you cannot have this kind of people in church and not have church hurt.

There are people that have gotten hurt in church because we may never have shown them love and care when they came, or when they told us about the problems they were going through. This is at all levels, from the mere member, to the ushers, the leaders and to the pastor. Some people have even left church because unlike the church folk, the people in the world have shown them love and care. It is very common and easy to send love through words only to somebody who is sick at home or in hospital, or someone who is going through emotional stress, marital problems, financial problems, or has a funeral. It must be emphasized that love and care must be genuine and practical.

With today's technology advancement, communication with people is just on phone and mostly without any physical and practical help whatsoever. We have made it a common habit to send our condolences on phone texts to members that have funerals rather than being there physically with them to offer them emotional help and any other help.

Love and care must be genuine, practical and meaningful.

> *"Don't pretend to love others. Really love them… Love each other with genuine affection, and take delight in honoring each other… When God's people are in need, be ready to help them. Always be eager to practice hospitality… Be happy with those who are happy; and weep with those who weep"* (Rom 12:9,10,15 NLT)

When we have people in the church who only love and care about themselves and not what matters to Jesus (and what matters to Jesus is the welfare of His people), we will have church hurt.

*"If the Lord Jesus is willing, I hope to send
Timothy to you soon for a visit. Then he can cheer
me up by telling me how you are getting along. I
have no one else like Timothy, who genuinely
cares about your welfare. All others care only
about themselves and not what matters to Jesus
Christ"* (Philippians 2:19-21 NLT)

Genuine love and care go beyond words but
expresses our Christian faith and values through
actions that help people and make a difference in
their lives.

*"By this we know love, because He laid down His
life for us. And we also ought to lay down our lives
for the brethren. But whoever has this world's
goods, and sees his brother in need, and shuts up
his heart from him, how does the love of God abide
in him? My little children, let us not love in word
or in tongue, but indeed and truth"* (1 John 3:16-
18)

*"What good is it, dear brothers and sisters, if you
say you have faith but don't show it by your
actions? Can that kind of faith save anyone?
Suppose you see a brother or sister who has no
food or clothing, and you say, 'Good-bye and have
a good day; stay warm and eat well,' but then you*

don't give that person any food or clothing, what good does that do? So, you see faith by itself isn't enough. Unless it produces good deeds. It is dead and useless" (James 2:14-17 NLT)

Betrayal, slander, jealousy and other evil tendencies among church folk today have brought so much hurt to many. Every other time, we hear of hurts done to people by fellow church members and sometimes by their leaders through the alluded to behaviors.

The reality of the love of self, love of money and pleasure at the expense of love for God has overtaken many people in church today, and the express result is so much hurt done to others. For selfish tendencies such as gossip, jealousy, hate, treachery, strife, selfish ambition, pride, arrogance, boasting, fraud, sexual immorality by and large hurt others, and this is typical in today's church in these last days. The love of money is the root of all kinds of evil things. Because of the love for money, many are trading their Christian faith and values for evil things, and in the end causing hurt to themselves and others. Because of leaders who are greedy, love money and pleasure rather than God, we hear of reports of financial mismanagement in churches and many people that have made so much contributions are hurt. It is annoying that some leaders even use the same monies to advance their immoral lifestyles. This hurts those who make such financial contributions.

"For the love of money is a root of kinds of evil, for which some have strayed from the faith in their greediness, and pierced themselves through with many sorrows... Command those who are rich in this present age not to be haughty, nor to trust in uncertain riches but in the living God, who gives us richly all things to enjoy"

(1 Tim 6:10,17)

Just as David's greed and sexual misdemeanor must have caused so much hurt to Uriah's family and to many other people in Israel, the greed and sexual immorality of leaders in the church today; which is the fruit of love of self, love of money and love of pleasure at the expense of love for God; is really hurting many people.

Tragedies Under Church Jurisdictions

1. **Accidents at Church:** The church is no stranger to accidents. Accidents can happen anywhere. But when an accident happens at church many people fail to take it or to deal

with it. There are accidents that have happened at some churches like children being hurt while playing, a car hitting a child or an adult at church, some part of the church build collapsing and injuring people or even killing a person, somebody drowning in the water during a baptismal event and several other accidents that may happen during church building construction. Such happenings have brought so much hurt upon the victims and their families in the church. Questions have been asked as to why there may have not been somebody supervising and looking after children while they played, or why there wasn't a steward to direct vehicles properly. Questions of wanting to know if there was compromise in the building process of the church facility may arise in case of a building collapsing. People may ask what led to someday drowning during a baptismal service in the full view of church leaders. Some church leaders have even had to go through legal battles for supposed negligence in view of such occurrences.

2. **Deaths at Church:** Tragic deaths have happened at some churches. Some have

been individual deaths and deaths of masses have happened mostly through collapsing of church buildings. Other deaths have happened when vehicles run over some people while driving in or out of the church premises. Such happenings have left families of the deceased and even other church members with so much hurt. And equally church leaders have had to face legal battles to answer whether they had indirect or direct responsibility that caused death to their members. Many have developed hatred for the church after such unfortunate events. Unsaved relatives have hardened their hearts towards the gospel and the church after losing their loved ones in church premises. Sometimes myths and misconceptions have arisen in such times with people accusing some church leaders of practicing satanism or witchcraft.

3. **Accidents and Deaths on Church Mission Trips:** In their commitment to church events, some people have suffered accidents, and some Christians have died as they travelled to and from church. Others have had road fatal traffic accidents while they

went on church mission trips. Such unfortunate events bring so much hate on the victims, their loved ones, and even other friends in the church. Consequently, most victims, families and friends of the victims have blamed the church and its leadership for their fate. When people are hurt, they look for someone to blame. Many have ended up blaming the church and subsequently God. Many people have an assumption that bad things such as tragedies cannot happen to people who are truly serving God.

4. **Death During Religious Tourism:** Religious tourism is when people visit a place they see as a holy place; for example, Israel. Other Christians see certain mega church as 'holy land' and they will make it a point to travel from all over the world to visit these mega churches. Other churches have designed certain portions of their church property as holy mountains, holy water pools, or places of experiencing divine contact for miracles. I keep imagining how one can evangelize to an unbelieving husband who may have discouraged his wife

to go on a 'religious tour' and yet she wouldn't listen to him, but went and unfortunately died in an accident. I imagine the pain and hatred they feel towards the named church. Think about the unbelieving relatives, children or how parents felt about the church when they heard of the news of their loved ones dying on a 'religious tour'. These people experience a certain pain you might not understand. When you hear them talk about how much they don't want anything to do with the church, you would be seriously touched. Such people really need God's special intervention for them to be healed.

5. **Failed or Unfulfilled Prophecies:** Scripture says "hope deferred makes the heart sick" (Prov 13 vs 12).When you are promised something and it doesn't happen, it saddens and depresses your heart. Many have been hurt in church owing to unfulfilled prophecies. They have felt they were lied to. Whenever prophecies are released and are delayed or not fulfilled, many have been hurt and left church. We will discuss this point further in the next chapters.

6. **Divorce:** One of the painful experiences one may go through in life is divorce. Issues surrounding divorce can bring a lot of hurt. Through divorce the couple, their children and those that are related to them can be very hurt. Some children may blame themselves whenever their parents'divorce and some children may even feel a sense of abandonment from either of their parents. The breaking of marriages in churches especially that of pastors, elders and church leaders hurts. To think of your pastor who has been publicly praising his wife and saying how God told him to marry her and now they are going separate ways is not an easy pill to swallow. The rampant rate of divorce among our spiritual role models has been a great source of church hurt today. The divorce of your spiritual leader is as painful as the divorce of your biological parents.

7. **Sexual Abuse:** Sexual abuse on a church member by a leader or any other fellow member can be very tragic and traumatizing. There are people that have been hurt in

church through sexual rape, including children that have suffered sexual defilement. Some prayer sessions turned out to be rape scenarios. Victims of rape and their family members carry in their hearts pain you will never understand.

Perhaps you may be a victim of any of these types church hurt. You lost a family member, friend, loved one and it has been so hard for you to let go and receive healing? Or any other I may not have mentioned, believe me, Only Jesus Christ can heal your broken heart and restore you. Church people may not have hurt supported you enough or stand by your side while mourning. It's so unfortunate, but I want you to know that God is no short of healing for the most broken hearts and spirits. Through his grace and power, he will heal and restore you if will only allow Him.

Church Systems, Protocols and Structures

Without systems and structures, the church cannot excel and thrive to its greatest potentials. I have a master's degree in leadership and that helped me to gain great understanding when it comes to the importance for developing systems and church leadership structures for the smooth running of the church. God has gifted some individuals with the gift of administration (Rom 12:7). However, I have to admit that some church systems have not met some practical needs of people they are developed to serve.

I served in a mega ministry and countless times I saw people suffer, die while following certain church protocols. I strongly believe systems and protocols are put in place to serve people's needs in an orderly manner. If church systems don't have service to people as its reason for their existence, then their aim is misguided.

A certain pastor left a ministry because he was suddenly dropped from the list of those who were supposed to be sent out as branch pastors outside the country. He had quit his job together with his wife, sold some of his property, and prepared everything to travel to this new country but about a week or two before travelling, some top church leaders manipulated the system and he was dropped. The senior pastor could not do anything about it in honor of the system and that's how they lost him.

Of course, certain individuals have a tendency to always go against systems and protocols put in place. Others have the tendency of manipulating church systems in ways that favor them or the people they like. That's disrespectful and it should not be tolerated. Church systems must help and serve people.

CHAPTER4
WHO IS BEHIND CHURCH HURT?

"And I, brethren, could not speak to you as to spiritual people but as to carnal, as to babes in Christ. I fed you with milk and not with solid food; for until now you were not able to receive it, and even now you are still not able; for you are still carnal. For where there are envy, strife, and divisions among you, are you not carnal and behaving like mere men?"

(1 Cor 3:1-3)

The State of Confusion

In my quest to understand and discover why people have become so hurt by the church, I have come to ask this question "Who is really behind church hurt?" What is the spirit and the force that is causing people all over the world to continuously experience hurt every time they came near the church? It seems like the further you are from church, the better for you. When you are nowhere near church there will be no pressure, no fights, no confusions, no church drama, no church politics, etc. When you are far from church, church issues are far from you; so it seems.

The church is supposed to be the place where people find clarity, direction and peace but the opposite seems to be true for many. This confusion disorients even the most intelligent and brilliant people. When you are confused, you are thrown into uncertainty. Confusion comes to rob you of the clarity of the importance of church in your life. When you are confused, you don't clearly see why you need to belong to a church. You begin to ask yourself, "if this is really the house of God, why am I being so hurt in God's holy house?" Reconciling the love of God and the hurt we experience in God's house can be confusing.

Confusion may vary in levels and degrees but its impact on one's Christian life is evident. Whenever you are confused about something, it's natural for you to withdraw and focus on the areas where you have clarity of purpose.

The Impact of Confusion

The church is supposed to be the light in the world, but it seems the light is deemed and there is a lot of confusion among us. We have constantly argued on doctrines, teachings, and recently the prophetic movement has initiated an unhealthy competition of who is the greatest? – A fight for supremacy among the clergy.

The church unfortunately is in a state of confusion. We are not clear on our message, mission, priorities and our core business. Every denomination clearly has its own agenda. Today we constantly see one church fighting another, one prophet or pastor is busy fighting another. The confusion among church leaders spreads to the followers and disorients them. The church at Corinth was one such example of a very gifted church but full of confusion inflamed by envy, strife, divisive tendencies among the church members. That kind of environment disoriented the members that it brought about division in the church.

Confusion comes to stir up strife, arguments, quarrels, discord and many other hurtful behaviors that eventually make people withdraw from church.Whatever God does, He will not use confusion in anyway. Even if God wants you to leave and move to another church, He won't use confusion to do so. He is not the author of confusion. The spirit of confusion is responsible for many hurts in the church.

"For God is not the author of confusion but of peace, as in all the churches of the saints" (1 Cor 14:33)

The Spirit of Confusion

Confusion is one dreadful evil spirit that brings great damage to the Body of Christ. I strongly believe if we can fully expose this spirit in the church and be on alert, it will become weaker and weaker and we will save many people from falling away from the house of God.

This spirit of confusion releases another spirit, a 'party spirit' to further perpetuate its agenda to weaken the church. This is the mother of all church politics and divisions. The church becomes a meeting center for each "church political party" and church members are turned into boot leaking church cadres instead of being dedicated disciples of Jesus Christ. Church members begin taking sides with whoever they think is the greatest of the ministers of God instead of focusing on the greatness of Jesus. Jesus should be the center and the core of our faith and Christian values. The "party spirit" has robbed the church of its commitment to Jesus Christ and reduced believers into senseless cadres of their spiritual fathers/mothers.

*"**For you are still carnal. For where there are envy, strife, and divisions among you, are you not carnal and behaving like mere men?** For one says, "I am of Paul," and another, "I am of Apollos," are you not carnal? Who then is Paul, and who is Apollos, but ministers through whom you believed, as the Lord gave each one?... For no other foundation can anyone lay than that which is laid, which is Jesus Christ"* (1 Cor 3:3-5,11).

Confusion and all kinds of evil, including every tendency that bring so much hurt in people right in church have a demonic source. Just like he caused confusion and division in heaven and was thrown out with his rebellious angels, Satan has the same agenda today, and is bent at bringing confusion among the brethren.

*"But if you have **bitter envy and self-seeking in your hearts**, do not boast and lie against the truth. This wisdom does not descend from above, **but is earthly, sensual, demonic**. For where envy and self-seeking exist, **confusion** and every evil thing are there"*

(James 3:14-16)

Confusion springs from a spirit of jealousy and selfish ambition. God never authors confusion. Fallen mankind is naturally selfish and this becomes the foundation upon which the spirit of confusion begins to bring all kinds of things that hurt people in the church. Everybody seems to just be about driving their selfish agenda and taking advantage of other people. The human tendency to be greedy and selfish is what normally breeds confusion even among the believers.

There were ministers at the time of Paul who preached the gospel without being sincere and out of envy, strife and selfish ambition in order to hurt him. Imagine preaching to cause confusion and preaching to offend and hurt somebody? This is true in today's church. Some preach out of envy and jealous with clear intent to hurt other preachers and not really to point people to Jesus.

*"**Some indeed preach Christ even from envy and strife**, and some also from goodwill. The former preach Christ from **selfish ambition, not sincerely, supposing to add affliction to mychains**; but the latter out of love...."* (Philippians 1:15-18)

The antidote to confusion and self-seeking is selfless love, which does not seek its own interests but the interest of others. Selfless love does not seek to esteem oneself better than others. This kind of love seeks the wellbeing of other people.

"All things are lawful for me, but not all things are helpful; all things are lawful for me, but not all things edify. Let no one seek his own, but each one the other's well-being"

(1 Cor 10:23-24)

"Let nothing be done through selfish ambition or conceit, but in lowliness of mind let each esteem others better than himself. Let each of you look out not only for his own interests, but also for the interests of others"

(Philippians 2:3-4)

Mind your own business

One reason the spirit of confusion incites hurt in the church is because people won't mind their own business when they come to church. We have a church full of people who are busybodies spreading false rumors and gossip. Gossip has hurt more people in church than anything else you can ever think of. Gossip inflames discord and confusion in church. You may have been hurt and you left a church because somebody gossiped about you.

> *"...But we urge you, brethren, that you increase more and more; that you also aspire to lead a quiet life, **to mind your own business**, and to work with your own hands, as we commanded you..."*

(1 Thess 4:9-12)

When you do not know your purpose and have nothing to do, you become a busybody that would start going around gossiping and spreading confusion among the brethren.

> *"For we hear that there are some who walk among you in a disorderly manner, not working at all, but are busybodies"*

(2 Thess 3:11)

A busybody is someone who interferes with others; one who is nosy, intrusive or meddlesome; a meddler and one who won't mind his own business. Unfortunately, we have a lot of meddlers, gossipers, nosy and intrusive people in church who won't stay in their own lane and focus on their own business but have feet that areswift to spread gossip rather than the gospel. Peter was once a busybody and was silenced by Jesus.

"...Jesus said to him, 'Feed My sheep. Most assuredly, I say to you, when you were younger, you girded yourself and walked where you wished; but when you are old, you will stretch out your hands, and another will gird you and carry you where you do not wish.' This He spoke, signifying by what death he would glorify God. And when He had spoken this, He said to him, 'Follow Me.' **Then Peter, turning around, saw the disciple whom Jesus loved following, who also had leaned on His breast at the supper, and said, 'Lord, who is the one who betrays You?'** *Peter seeing him, said to Jesus,* **'But Lord, what about this man?' Jesus said to him, 'If I will that he remains till I come, what is that to you? You follow Me"**

(John 21:17-22)

People come to church through the gospel, and they leave because of gossip. Beware of gossipers when you go to church They are agents of the spirit of confusion that bring hurt to many in church.

CHAPTER 5

THE COST OF CHURCH HURT

"Then after some days Paul said to Barnabas, 'Let us now go back and visit our brethren in every city where we have preached the word of the Lord, and see how they are doing.' Now Barnabas was determined to take with them John called Mark.

But Paul insisted that they should not take him with them one who had departed from them in Pamphylia and had not gone with them to the work. Then the contention became so sharp they parted from one another. And so Barnabas took Mark and sailed to Cyprus; but Paul chose Silas and departed being commended by the brethren to the grace of God. And he went through Syria and Cilicia, strengthening the churches"

(Acts 15:36-41)

"Only Luke is with me. Get Mark and bring him with you, for he is useful to me for ministry"

(2 Tim 4:11)

Believe it or not, the impact of church hurt on believers is immensely outrageous. Most people who leave church have no problem with God. People have a problem with the church organization. They have a problem with their fellow human beings in the church organization. We should not under-estimate the power of church hurt. Here are a few things church hurt will do:

1. Discouragement

Church hurt brings you to a place of constant discouragement. You will be discouraged from continuing to do the work of God within the corners of the church because of what has happened to you in church. You will rather decide to either stay home or remain idle and not involve yourself in any church activity. Discouragement incapacitates one's strength to continue working tirelessly for God.

Due to church hurt, we have people that have become so discouraged that they even left church for the world. They feel that in the world they are treated right and better than they were by church folk.

2. Depression

It is sad to say that some people have never been so depressed until they entered the doors of church. From the young to the old, the levels of depression people experience in church is alarming. A place that is supposed to be a source of rest and comfort has turned out to be a place where others have gotten the most depressing moments of their lives. This is so sad because the issues of depression of believers are actually coming from among themselves.

People get discouraged when they are mistreated by their fellow believers. Many are suffering the mental illness of depression and some are even suicidal because of some rumor or gossip about them from some fellow church members. We shall discuss this in detail a bit later.

3. Loss of Church Workers

In Mathew 9:37, the Lord Jesus says *"the harvest is plenteous but the laborers are few"*. As a result of church hurt, we have lost amazing people who were working very well in God's house. Those who had given themselves to serve the Lord have left the church because of bitter experiences within the church. While the Lord is looking for laborers in the vineyard, church hurt is causing some people to depart the Lord's field.

Church hurt is responsible for the loss of great giftings and resources. Resourceful people have been lost to the world. Some of the young people we see singing non gospel music and lost in the world were once part of the church but because nobody understood them and supported their talent, they left. When they went to the world, they were received with both hands. Such could have been a great resource to the church in advancing the kingdom of God, but the judgmental attitude hurt them away from the kingdom.

4. Backsliding

Others have gone back to the world after experiencing hurt in church. I know a lady leader who had gone through some church hurt and to this day she has refused to return to church. Her church hurt experience is the reason for her backsliding. You may say she was not truly saved or was not serious with God in the first place, but one thing I have come to understand is that church hurt can sometimes make you do things you never thought you would ever do in your life. Backsliding is one of the costs of church hurt. People slide back to doing the things of the world because they feel that the church is actually more hostile than the world which they find friendly.

Most people would have never left church for the world, but the hurt they experienced in the church was too much that they could not stay. Some people have backslidden because they were shown constant condemnation from the church folk. When people are not shown patience to grow in their Christian walk with the Lord, it has the potential to discourage them from attending church. They feel hurt and consequently they abandon their local church.

5. Loss of Zeal for the work of God

If there is something that I have noticed to a massive killer of zeal in the work of the ministry is church hurt. When you are hurting, you have no practical zeal for anything. In Titus 2:14, we see that our Lord Jesus *"...gave Himself for us, that He might redeem us from iniquity, and purify unto himself a peculiar people, **zealous of good works**."* In Christ's agenda of redemption, the end result is to have you and I zealous for good works for the Lord.

Zeal for God is killed when you constantly experience church hurt. Especially those who are fully grounded and rooted in the ministry, they have been the greatest victims of loss of zeal. When you see a "once upon a time zealous believer" now cold and cannot get up to do anything for God, you have to drag them and force them to serve in the ministry. At the root of this loss of zeal is church hurt.

6. Broken Ministry Partnerships

Through church hurt great ministry partnerships have been broken down. People who were going to do great things working together for the kingdom end up separating on the platform of church hurt.

We have a record in church history about the sharp conflict that the ministry partners, Paul and Barnabas had concerning John Mark. The two apostles were to go back to visit the believers whom they had won to Christ but Barnabas (as the son of encouragement) still insisted that John Mark be part of their mission. Paul was too hurt to have John Mark on the team again. Their previous mission trip had been with so much persecution on them that the young man John Mark abandoned them on the mission field and would not continue with them in the work of the ministry. This made Paul feel that John Mark was not a dependable person to have in the team. However, Barnabas, like his name was "Son of encouragement" thought otherwise; he probably thought the young man needed time to grow in the ministry. The argument became so sharp that the two great apostles ended up separating from each other. Barnabas went, taking John Mark with him and sailed to Cyprus and Paul took Silas and left for Syria and Cilicia. From that time, we don't hear of Barnabas. What was a great apostolic partnership ended with that sharp hurtful contention and separation.

"Then after some days Paul said to Barnabas, 'Let us now go back and visit our brethren in every city where we have preached the word of the Lord, and see how they are doing." Now Barnabas was determined to take with them John called Mark. But Paul insisted that they should not take with

(Acts 15:36-41)

7. Church Break-Away

Church hurt is one of the leading causes of church splits and breakaways. Very few people leave former churches happy. At the core of most church breakaways is church hurt.

Furthermore, church hurt is responsible for the emerging of most independent ministries, and Christian organizations that have no connection to any church denomination. One may be called to serve under a ministry but once they experience hurt, they end up forming independent ministries.

Did you know that church hurt even has the potential to change somebody's message forever? Most ministers that were hurt in church and left to establish their own independent ministries and never dealt with their pain usually express their hurt and bitterness in their message and ministration. You cannot effectively minister with a foundation of bitterness and hurt.

A bitter minister through his messages will end up defiling and poisoning his flock with his attitude. Bitterness is like poison. It has the potential to destroy a healthy Christian life. We should *"Pursue peace with all people, and holiness, without which no one will see the Lord; looking carefully lest anyone fall short of the grace of God; lest any root of bitterness springing up cause trouble, and by this many become defiled"* (Hebrew 12:14-15)

8. Stagnation of the Church

Church hurt is one of the subtle weapons in the devil's armory to weaken, devastate and destabilize the progressive of Christian ministries. Because of church hurt, church growth, church influence and church expansion has been put to a place of limitation. The people who are supposed to be used by God in the expansion of His kingdom at large are stuck in church hurt. When church hurt happens at the leadership level, it has the potential to stop the progress and growth of the church family. When Miriam and Aaron gossiped about Moses and God rebuked, warned and cautioned them, and struck Miriam with Leprosy for 7 days as a kind of discipline for their misconduct, the progress of the congregation was affected. The whole congregation could not move forward until the things were resolved.

*"So the anger of the Lord was aroused against them, and He departed. And when the cloud departed from above the tabernacle, suddenly Miriam became leprosy, as white as snow. Then Aaron turned toward Miriam, and there she was, a leper. So Aaron said to Moses, 'Oh, my lord! Please do not lay this sin on us, in which we have done foolishly and in which we have sinned. Please do not let her be as one dead, whose flesh is half consumed when he comes out of his mother's womb! So Moses cried out to the Lord, saying, 'Please heal her, O God, I pray!' Then the Lord said to Moses, 'If her father had but spit in her face, would she not be shamed seven days? Let her be shut out of the camp seven days, and afterward she may be received again. So Miriam was shut out of the camp seven days, **and the people did not journey till Miriam was brought again**"* (Num 12:9-16).

9. Shame and Ridicule of the Church

The five-fold ministry is no longer in a place of admiration and honor. Today the most spitefully talked about people are the clergy. The shame and ridicule have extended to the entire church. Moral failure, especially related to sex and finances has brought hurt in the church and made the church and the gospel to be evil spoken of, maligned and defamed.

*"**And many will follow their immoral ways and lascivious doings; because of them the true Way will be maligned and defamed**. And in their covetousness (lust, greed) they will exploit you with false (cunning) arguments. From of old the sentence of condemnation for them has not been idle; their destruction (eternal misery) has not been asleep "(2 Pet 2:2-3 Amplified)*

10. Hardening of Unbelievers' Hearts

Unbelievers' hearts have been hardened by the stories they hear from the people who are involved in the church. Many could have responded to the gospel and joined the church but the hurting stories they have heard from church folk and painful experiences some have literally seen church people go through has hardened and repelled them off.

The good news carriers are hurting. The evangelists are hurting. The preachers are hurting and they have a painful story to tell. The unbelieving listeners are hearing their plight. This makes it very difficult for the unbelievers to positively respond to the gospel. Unbelievers have always referred to the disunity and fights among Christians as a major discouraging factor for joining the faith.

Logically, nobody wants to join a traumatizing and hurtful society. You will naturally distance yourself from it regardless of its other benefits. Though none believers may not be aware of the great need for salvation, they will prefer to stay away from church hurt. The enemy has used church hurt to keep their hearts hardened and keep them away from church.

Lessons from Esau and Jacob

Though it was God's choice to pass on the Abrahamic blessing to Jacob, Isaac unknowingly but prophetically blessed Jacob instead of Esau. Jacob had taken away Esau's birth right and now the blessing. Filled with bitterness, Esau vowed to kill Jacob. Esau was hurt and he felt betrayed cheated not only by Jacob but by his parents, especially his mother who had colluded with Jacob to supplant him of the blessing. The hurt he experienced made him angry, bitter and caused him to begin plotting to murder his brother Jacob. However, Esau had great respect for his father, and so his plan was to wait until the death of his father before executing it. He would not want his father see him killing Jacob.

"So, Esau hated Jacob because of the blessing with which he had blessed him, and Esau said in his heart, 'The days of mourning for my father are at hand; then I will kill my brother Jacob" (Gen 27:41)

Esau went ahead and married two heathen wives against his father's advice. These women became a grief of heart to his parents. Being hurt and having seen and known how marrying heathen wives was a pain to his parents, he decided to marry a third wife to please and win his father's favor, for he thought perhaps that would reverse his fate. Hebrews refers to Esau as a fornicator because of his act of selling his birthright for a bowl of soap.

"Lest there be any fornicator or profane person like Esau, who for one morsel of food sold his birthright. For you know that afterward, when he wanted to inherit the blessing, he was rejected, for he found no place for repentance, though he sought it diligently with tears" (Hebrews 12:16-17).

"When Esau was forty years old, he took as wives Judith the daughters of Beeri the Hittite, and Basemath the daughter of Elon the Hittite. ***And they were a grief of mind to Isaac and Rebekah"*** (Gen 26:34-35).

He went ahead to add more wives, and he married one from Ishmael, Abraham's son, in order to appease his father.

"Also Esau saw that the daughters of Canaan did not please his father Isaac. So Esau went to Ishmael and took Mahalath, the daughter of Ishmael, Abraham's son, the sister of Naboioth, to be his wife in addition to the wives he had" (Gen 28:8-9).

Esau is painted in bad light by many Bible scholars and preachers, but he turns out to be a man with a big heart. He was hurt but he forgave his brother Jacob and reconciled with him in the end. The story ends well because even when their father died, the two sons were there together to bury him.

"Now the days of Isaac were one hundred and eighty years. So Isaac breathed his last and died, and was gathered to his people, being old and full of days. And his sons Esau and Jacob buried him" (Gen 35:28-29).

The story of Esau and Jacob teaches us lessons of how we can forgive, reconcile and heal from hurt and the separation that we may have experienced due to confusion and a "party spirit" in the church. Esau has shown us the right way.

CHAPTER 6

FALSEHOOD IN THE CHURCH

"But there were also false prophets in Israel just as there will be false teachers among you. They will cleverly teach destructive heresies and even deny the Master who bought them. In this way, they will bring sudden destruction on themselves. Many will follow their evil teaching and shameful immorality. And because of these teachers, the Way of Truth will be slandered. In their greed they will make up clever lies to get hold of your money. But God condemned them long ago, and their destruction will not be delayed"

(2 Pet 2:1-3 NLT)

Falsehood refers to untruthfulness, fabrication of lies, half-truths and so on. The discovery of falsehood that exits in the church today has brought many to a place of church hurt.

The scriptures record numerous passages where God is warning us to be careful about falsehood and be watchful of the people whose agenda is to publish falsehood. Falsehood has the potential to cause hurt to another and to destroy peace.

"The hypocrite with his mouth destroys his neighbor..." (Prov 11:9)

"Keep your tongue from evil, and your lips from speaking deceit. Depart from evil and do good; seek peace and pursue it" (Ps 34:13-14)

The extent to which people in the church can participate in falsehood is very shocking. People in the church today are able to bare false witness against each other as though they are not brothers and sisters in the Lord. One can stand up and fabricate a completely false accusation. They can narrate it so well that everyone is fooled. I have been a victim of false fabrications from the people I pastored and prayed for.

I remember as a young single pastor, I was serving in one of the churches as a resident pastor. I then decided to change the leadership of the church. Among the changes I made was the church treasurer. I appointed another lady to take up the financial department. This decision did not sit well with a few people in the former church leadership and they formed up a group - a kind of pressure groupand began to fabricate all forms of false stories about me. The story that really shocked me was when I heard that I had madethe new church treasurer pregnant. I couldn't believe that the people I was praying for and preaching to every Sunday would falsely accuse me of such. Now this lady had been trusting God for a child with her husband for a while. When I then appointed her as the new treasurer, she also fell pregnant about the same time. My accusers took advantage of the situation and made up a story to destroy my reputation.

I had been so discouraged and depressed at that point of my life and I couldn't understand why someone would boldly start spreading such kind of falsehood especially about their pastor. I think that was one of my most difficult times I had gone through in ministry. Preaching in front of people who were falsely accusing me was unbearable, but God gave me grace.

Men and women of God have in the recent past gone through numerous false accusations that are unbearable. It has become so easy to falsely accuse a pastor especially those who have broken through internationally. Most of these false accusations are spread by fellow clergy men and women. This reality is very painful. As the saying goes "the enemy of a pastor is a pastor". It is a sad sight to see.

Now on the other hand, falsehood in the church has made many leave the church. There are some who have seen fake miracles, fake testimonies, fake healings, fake prophecies and many other fake things advanced by false clergymen. Someone told me how they were prophesied to and prior to the prophecy they had been briefed on how they were supposed to respond and answer. These are staged prophecies. People get hurt when their first encounter with the church is falsehood.

Today, people do not believe in the power of God because they have seen leading names in the church fake miracles. The Bible warns us to beware of falseprophets: *"And Jesus answered and said, 'Take heed that no one deceives you. For **many will come in my name,** saying, 'I am Christ, and will **deceive many.'**... Then **many false prophets** will rise up and **deceive many"*** (Matt 24:4,5,11).

Many! Not a few of them, but many would be deceived! Apostle Paul also warns the church: *"For the time is coming when people will not tolerate (endure) sound and wholesome instruction, but having ears itching for something pleasing and gratifying, they will gather to themselves **one teacher after another to a considerable number**, chosen to satisfy their own liking and foster the errors they hold. And will turn aside from hearing the truth and wander off into **myths** and man-made**fictions"*** (2 Tim 4:3-4 Amplified)

We are now living in the times of these prophetic utterances of Apostle Paul. A time has come when we are seeing this reality. A time has come when people in the Christian world no longer tolerate the sound teaching of God's word. Many people have itching ears for something to satisfy their selfish desires and to empower them to foster the errors they already hold. Further, they gather for themselves, many false teachers and preachers, specifically chosen for that objective, and because of that, they have turned aside, wondered off the Truth of God's word and have made themselves vulnerable and victims of themselves to myths and fables.

A **Myth** is a commonly-held false belief which people treat as true. It is a common misconception; a fictitious or imaginary person or thing; it is a person or thing held in excessive, quasi-religious awe or admiration based on popular legend (story of unknown origin describing extraordinary past events).

Today we have people spreading falsehood in form of myths through false prophesies and false teachings. What they preach and teach, unfortunately, are being held with such awe and admiration by the larger section of the church, even if those things are nothing but falsehoods.

A **<u>fable</u>** is a fictitious narrative intended to enforce some instruction or concept. It is a story told to excite wonder, a man-made fiction, untruth and falsehood.

Today, the church has been invaded by false prophets because, typical masquerades and actors, bringing fictitious teachings and fabricated practices. Fake miracles and prophesies have become the order of the day. Some so called miracles are merely stage-managed activities to mesmerize the patrons. False prophets enforce their false teachings and ideas by using stories and actions which they know will stimulate wonder and awe in the audience.

When the cap of deception is off the people's heads, and they discover that they were subjected to"myths" and the "fictions"they become hurt. Some have left church after discovering that they under a spell of deception.

Apostle Paul wrote to the Corinthian church: *"For we are not, like **so many (like hucksters making a trade of) peddling God's word,** (short-changing and adulterating the divine message); but like men of sincerity and purest motive, as commissioned and sent by God, we speak His message in Christ* *(the Messiah) in the very sight and presence of God"* (2 Cor 2:17 Amplified)

That is so alarming, and we are seeing this reality even today. We have so many false prophets exploiting gullible people. We have many out there who are short-changing God's word and watering it down by it as a means for making money, literary turning the people who sit under them into business franchises.

Apostle Paul also wrote to Titus his son in the faith *"For there are **many disorderly and unruly men who are idle (vain, empty) and misleading and self-deceivers and deceivers of others**. This is true, especially of those of the circumcision party (who come over from Judaism). **Their mouths must be stopped, for they are mentally distressing and subverting whole families by teaching what they ought not to teach,** for the purpose of getting base advantage and disreputable gain. One of their very number, a prophet of their own, said, **Cretans are always liars, hurtful beasts**, idle and lazy gluttons. And this account of them is really true. Because it is true, rebuke them sharply (deal sternly, even severely with them), so that they may be sound in their faith and flee from error, and may show their soundness by ceasing to give attention to Jewish* *myths and fables or to rules laid down by mere men who reject and turn their backs on the Truth"* (Titus 1:10-14).

You see how falsehood is also responsible for mental illness in the church today. Many people are distressed and are hurting today in the church because of falsehood. False prophesies and false teachings based on the greed of the false ministers is responsible for much of the mental illness in the church today. We will deal with the subject of church hurt and mental health later as we progress.

False Teachers

Notice that Paul quoted what one of their own prophets said about those false ministers in the Cretan church: he said "Cretans are liars, hurtful beasts…", and Paul said that account was actually true about them. Falsehood brings church hurt. Falsehood brings mental illness in the church.This is how words can mentally distress and hurt people so badly.

Apostle Peter said just as there were false prophets in Israel in old times, there would be false teachers in the church who would shrewdly introduce destructive teachings, for the purpose of exploiting the people of their money. He said those teachers will be so immoral in teaching and conduct and many, not a few, but many people in the church will follow their false teachings and shameful immorality. He said those teachers will have a lifestyle of sin and sexual immorality, and they will entice unstable souls. They would promise freedom but they themselves are in bondage with immorality. They would be responsible for much of the corruption and immorality in the church by their false teachings, and immoral conduct.

"But there were also false prophets among the people, even as there will be false teachers among you, who will secretly bring in destructive heresies, even denying the Lord who bought them, and bring on themselves swift destruction. And many will follow their destructive ways, because of whom the way of truth will be blasphemed... having eyes full of adultery and that cannot cease from sin, enticing unstable souls. They have a heart trained in covetous practices, and are accursed children. They have forsaken the right way and gone astray, following the way of Balaam the son of Boer, who loved the wages of unrighteousness... While they promise them liberty, they themselves are slaves of corruption" (2 Per 2:1,2,14,15,19).

We are seeing the reality of Apostle Peter's prophetic utterances in today's church. We are seeing ministers who were once sound teachers of God's word turning into false teachers and false prophets because of greed for money. We are seeing many ministers going the way of Balaam the son of Boer who loved the rewards of money, to the point of teaching Balak son of Zippor to ensnare the children of Israel by causing them to break their covenant with God.

The quest to make merchandise of people has even given rise to the selling of emblems and substances that are believed to have miraculous powers to help people, such as "anointed bracelets, anointed soaps, anointed brooms, anointing water, among others". Anointing oil is also highly abused by the false teachers and prophets.

False Prophets

Jesus said many false prophets shall rise and deceive many: *"Then **many false prophets** will rise up and deceive many"* (Matt 24:11). Apostle John warned the church at Ephesus, *"Beloved, do not believe every spirit, but test the spirits whether they are of God; **because many false prophets*** *have gone out into the world. By this you know the Spirit of God: every spirit that confesses that Jesus Christ has come in the flesh is of God, and every spirit that does not confess that Jesus Christ has come in the flesh is not of God. And this is the spirit of the antichrist, which you have heard was coming, and is now already in the world"* (1 John 4:1-3)

Many people are deceived, destabilized, exploited and suffering. Presently, there is a great rise of a great number of "prophets", and the competition among them is rife. We are even hearing reports of who is the greatest among them. There are prophesies and words of knowledge that are man-made that have disturbed and hurt many people. There are some people suffering mental illnesses and broken relationships and marriages in church today because of this falsehood.

There are reports of some prophets deceiving women in the church to have sex with them, and they abuse scripture to justify their actions. We hear of some propagating that just as Sarah suggested to her husband Abraham to have her maid Hagar as a concubine, so a prophet's wife may suggest to her husband who he should have sex with. They insist that there is nothing wrong with the prophet having extra-marital affairs as long as it's within the house (church). They twist the story of Abraham and Sarah in which Sarah suggested that Abraham should take Hagar for a concubine. This heresy has hurt many women that are devoid of truth. They have been manipulated and abused sexually by the false prophets. Many frustrated and hurting women have vowed never to return to church again on account the emotional they experienced after being sexually abused by the false prophets.

*"But understand this, that in the last days will come (set in) perilous **times of great stress** and trouble **(hard to deal with and hard to bear)**. For people will be lovers of self and utterly self-centered, lovers of money and aroused by inordinate greedy desire for wealth... they will be treacherous betrayers, rash and inflated with self-conceit, they will be lovers of pleasures and vain amusements more than and rather than lovers of God. For although they hold a form of piety (true religion), they deny and reject and strangers to the power of it (their conduct belies the genuineness of their profession). Avoid all such people (turn away from them). For among them are those who worm their way into homes and captivate silly and weak-*

natured and spiritually dwarfed women, loaded down with the burden of their sins and easily swayed and led away by various evil desires and seductive impulses. These weak women will listen to anybody who will teach them; they are forever inquiring and getting information, but are never able to arrive at a recognition and knowledge of the Truth" (2 Tim 3:1,2,4-9 Amplified)

False
Apostles

Jesus appeared to Apostle John and He began to instruct him to write letters to the seven churches. One of the churches He told him to right to was the church of Ephesus. This church had started well and was devoted to Christ, but with the passing of time it abandoned its first love for the Lord and was no longer doing the first works it used to do. Jesus wrote to rebuke this church and to implore it to repent or He would remove its lampstand (influence and existence) from its place. However, the Lord said He was aware of some good works in the church and He commended them for it. He knew about their patience and labor in His name, and how they could not bear those who were evil, and how they had tested those who used to claim to be apostles but were not and had found them to be liars.

The church of Ephesus represented the section of the church today that has left its first love and is no longer serving the Lord as it should. However, though this was the picture of this church at Ephesus, the Lord had something good to say about them – they could not bear those who were evil and had tested those who were claiming to be apostles but were not and had found them to be liars. Even today, we have some people in the church claiming to be apostles but are actually not; they are but liars and deceivers.

*"To the angel of the church of Ephesus write, 'These things says He who holds the seven star in His right hand, who walks in the midst of the seven golden lampstands. I know your works, your labor, your patience, and that you cannot bear those who are evil. And you have tested those **who say they are apostles** and are not, and **have found them liars**"* (Rev 2:1-2).

Apostle Paul wrote to the church at Corinth where there were some ministers who were claiming to be "super-apostles" but were actually ministers of Satan. Those false apostles were preaching another kind of Christ, another kind of gospel and were imparting another kind of spirit on the believers rather than the Holy Spirit. There teachings and ministry corrupted the minds of the believers and turned them from their sincere devotion to Christ. The unfortunate thing is that the church had tolerated their shenanigans. They let them fool them, put them in bondage, exploit them, take advantage of them, trample upon them, abuse them and shame them to their face.

"I am jealous for you with a godly jealousy. I promised you to one husband, to Christ, so that I might present you as a pure virgin to Him. But I am afraid that just as Eve was deceived by the serpent's cunning, your minds may somehow be led astray from your sincere and pure devotion to Christ. For if someone comes to you and preaches a Jesus other than the Jesus we preached, or if you receive a different spirit from the Spirit you received, or a different gospel from the one you accepted, you put up with it easily enough. I don't think I am in the least inferior to those "super apostles" ... For such are people are false apostles, deceitful workers, masquerading as apostles of Christ. And no wonder, for Satan himself masquerades as an angel of light. It is not

surprising, then, if his servants also, masquerades as servants of righteousness. Their end will be what their actions deserve... You gladly put up with fools since you are so wise! In fact, you even put up with anyone who enslaves you or exploits you or takes advantage of you or puts on airs or slaps you in the face" (2 Cor 11:2-5,13-15,19,20 NIV)

False apostles, "super-apostles" as Paul would call them, foster teachings and practices that corrupt believers' minds and lead them astray from the sincere and pure devotion to Christ. They preach another kind of Jesus and a different type of gospel and impart another kind of spirit rather than the one revealed and characterized in Holy Scripture. False apostles fool people in the church, they enslave people, exploit people, take advantage of people, trample down people and shame people. This is so typical in the church today. We see this kind of church hurt coming because of false prophets, false teachers and false apostles.

False Doctrines

We are living in the times when people are departing from the Christian faith for deceiving spirits and things taught by demons, which come through hypocritical liars, whose consciences have been seared as with a hot iron.

All the teachings and practices in the church that is about forbidding people to marry or that control people by telling them who to marry and who not to marry, telling people to abstain from certain foods, telling people when to travel and when not to travel, among other emotional manipulations are deceptive and demonic. Such teachings and practices have enslaved and hurt many people in the church (We will deal with this later as we talk about religious enslavement).

*"The Spirit clearly says that in the later times some will abandon the faith and follow deceiving spirits and things taught by demons. **Such teachings come through hypocritical liars**, whose consciences have been seared as with a hot iron. They forbid people to marry and order them to abstain from certain foods, which God has created to be received with thanksgiving by those who believe and who know the truth. For everything God created is good and nothing is to be rejected if it received with thanksgiving, because it is consecrated by the word of God and prayer"* (1 Tim 4:1-10).

Some other false teachings are mythical and fictitious, and they are deliberately taught by hypocritical ministers to foster their evil agenda by exciting people to the point of being exploited of their money, taken advantage of, abused and hurt in the end.

I know that we have many ministers whose hearts are genuine, pure and really want to serve God in church. But in some cases, even genuine ministers have found themselves in situations they didn't initially intend to be in. I had such an experience before. Therefore, I know what I am talking about. Satan is aiming at deceiving people with the call of God so that many can be led astray through their influence. It's shameful and painful to realize that one followed falsehood. But we give God the glory for those who get restored. The bible says, *"For false Christs and false prophets will rise and show great signs and wonders to deceive, if possible, even the elect"* (Matt 24:24).

The deception of the enemy is real. It is his greatest strength and weapon. He deceived Eve in the garden and actually also tried to deceive Jesus in the wilderness. What audacity! Satan is the master of deception.

Please do not fall into a trap of generalizing and start calling everyone false or fake. At the same time do not believe everything and everyone. The Bible teaches us to test every spirit whether it be of God. Don't hate the prophetic ministry because of false prophets you have encountered. Don't hurt the apostolic ministry because of the false apostles you have encountered. Don't hate the teaching ministry because of the false teachers you have encountered. The Scriptures we have gone through were written to warn us about such people. You were adequately warned, you have been made aware of what is happening around the church fraternity beforehand.

I know how painful it is to realize that you were fooled when you thought you were clever and were under impression that you had everything under control. I know the sad feeling you get when have your eyes opened to the fact that someone was feeding you with lies and you swallowed everything like a helpless newly hatched bird. But thank God for not allowing you to continue believing in the lies. Your eyes are open now and you can see clearly. Be grateful that you got to know that it was fake. It may hurt that you were deceived, but appreciate the fact that by the grace of God you had received the discernment by the Spirit that gave you revelation of the truth. Instead of being bitter, be better. Instead of being hurt be happy. Be happy that you are free from the bondage of falsehood.

CHAPTER 7

HURT FROM THE PULPIT

"For you put up with it if one brings you into bondage, if one devours you, if one takes from you, if one exalts himself, if one strikes you on the face"
(2 Cor 11:20)

Pulpit hurt is the one you get from the clergy; that is from the pastor, prophet, priest or the preacher who ministers to you from the altar in your congregation. Sadly, most of us have been hurt terribly by the men and women God has ordained to take care of our spiritual welfare. I am aware there are individuals who I have hurt as a man on the pulpit. Being a Pastor, people have certain expectations from you and if you don't meet them, you will be shocked how much you have hurt them.

I had a certain member who left the church because I didn't visit the mother thetime, she was sick. Another one told me they left the church because I did not support them enough when they were getting married. Another left our church because I didn't give him opportunity to preach but rather gave another. Some ladies mobilized and left because they felt I strongly condemned women when I preached about evil women in the Bible in the likes of Jezebel, Delilah, Athaliah. I once heard some people got so hurt when I encouraged everyone to go to school and study or upgrade their qualifications, they felt hurt because they were not educated and so many instances. You will be shocked what hurts people. People in church are very sensitive.

Men and Women of God on the pulpit knowingly and unknowingly hurt the flock of Christ. Without pride, I have made it a norm to humbly apologize to any church member who feels I have hurt them in anyway. I always pray and ask the Lord for forgiveness, mercy and grace to lead His people without harming them in any way.

I strongly believe that no genuine man or woman of God will intentionally hurt the Lord's flock, but being human, they fall short and fail to meet everyone's expectations. It is also the duty of a pastor to strongly warn, rebuke or correct his congregation. Sometimes the man or woman of God must speak sharply and it will be inevitable to displease some people.

Having said that, it is unfortunate that I have to admit that the pulpit has put so many in great church hurt. I remember my mother telling me how her pastor used to preach about her issues and it was one of the reasons she left the church. Many people have gone through this experience where their pastor begins to indirectly preach about them. Sometimes, this has come out after the member has had counseling sessions with the pastor, only to hear what was shared with him in confidence from the pulpit.

I met a certain lady and I asked her how her church was doing.She told me she had left the church and was just staying home. I asked her what happened and she answered and said "I had shared some confidential issues I was going through to the pastor's wife, only to hear her indirectly preaching about me." I tried to talk to her, saying maybe she was just being too sensitive but she insisted that the pastor's wife had included her private issues in her sermon. Now, this lady is no longer zealous for the work of the Lord.

Another brother told me how when he had impregnated a lady and was made to stand up in church and undergo discipline. I said to him that it was right to be disciplined for your wrong actions but he further highlighted that after some time, another brother in the same church who had a better financial status had committed the same sin, but was not made to stand in church but his issue was secretly and privately handled. He was so hurt and left the church.

I remember when I was in the youth ministry when one of the ladies in our group had gotten pregnant. She was made to stand in front of the church by the pastor and was publicly rebuked, banned from participating in church choir until we see the fruits of repentance, he said. As I sat behind the piano, I saw the young girl weep in shame and that was the last time I ever saw her in church. Immediately after the service, a lady who had recently joined the church asked me, "Jeff, is this how you treat people in your church? I can't join your church", she said.

I do understand the place of church discipline in the house of God, we need it to keep order, purity and holiness. At the same time, it is important for the pastor and the leadership not to neglect the people being disciplined. We must always remember to correct people who fall into sin with meekness. Paul wrote in Galatians 6:1-2,

"Dear brothers and sisters, if another believer is overcome by some sin, you who are godly should gently and humbly help that person back onto the right path. And be careful not to fall into the same temptation yourself" (Gal 6:1-2 NLT)

In 2 Samuel Chapter 12:1-14, you will discover a story about a prophet who confronted King David over his sinful behavior of committing adultery with Bathsheba and killing Uriah in order to cover up his sins. Let us quickly read the story of how Prophet Nathan handled this issue.

"The Lord sent Nathan to David. When he came to him, he said, "There were two men in a certain town, one rich and the other poor. The rich man had a very large number of sheep and cattle, but the poor man had nothing except one little ewe lamb he had bought. He raised it, and it grew up with him and his children. It shared his food, drank from his cup and even slept in his arms. It was like a daughter to him.Now a traveler came to the rich man, but the rich man refrained from taking one of his own sheep or cattle to prepare a meal for the traveler who had come to him. Instead, he took the ewe lamb that belonged to the poor man and prepared it for the one who had come to him."David burned with anger against the

man and said to Nathan,"As surely as the Lord lives, the man who did this deserves to die! He must pay for that lamb four times over, because he did such a thing and had no pity." Then Nathan said to David, "You are the man! This is what the Lord, the God of Israel, says: 'I anointed you king over Israel, and I delivered you from the hand of Saul. I gave your master's house to you, and your master's wives into your arms. I gave you the house of Israel and Judah. And if all this had been too little, I would have given you even more. Why did you despise the word of the Lord by doing what is evil in his eyes? You struck down Uriah the Hittite with the sword and took his wife to be your own. You killed him with the sword of the Ammonites. Now, therefore, the sword will never depart from your house, because you despised me and took the wife of Uriah the Hittite to be your own.This is what the Lord says: 'Out of your own household I am going to bring calamity upon you. Before your very eyes I will take your wives and give them to one who is close to you, and he will lie with your wives in broad daylight. You did it in secret, but I will do this thing in broad daylight before all Israel.Then David said to Nathan, "I have sinned against the Lord."Nathan replied, "The Lord has taken away your sin. You are not

*going to die. But because by doing this you have
made the enemies of the Lord show utter contempt,
the son born to you will die."*

(2 Sam 12:1-14)

Notice how the prophet Nathan displayed great wisdom in conveying the message of the Lord to David who had fallen into sin. This is something the people in the prophetic ministry need to learn. Most of them have a tendency of revealing people's sins in public and instead of getting the person to the point of repentance, they are taken to the place of embarrassment. Instead of winning them back to walking with God, they are driven far away from God. Most of young people, new believers especially and weak believers walk away from church in great pain. Paul spoke about arrogant ministers who have an attitude to abuse, exploit and bring more bondage on people, and to cause hurt and embarrassment to them.

*"For you put up with it if one brings you into
bondage, if one devours you, if one takes from you,
if one exalts himself, if one strikes you on the face"*
(2 Cor 11:20)

As a minister one must emulate the character of God when dealing with the matters of sin and shame in the people that seek for help. When Adam and Even sinned and were hiding in their shame among shrubs, God came and covered their shame (nakedness) with an animal's skin that He had killed to atone for their sin. We must cover people's nakedness (shame) rather than expose them more shame.

"Also, for Adam and his wife the Lord made tunics of skin, and clothed them" (Gen 3:21)

In 2nd Samuel 12:16, David pleaded with God for the child. He fasted and went into his house and spent nights lying on the ground.

This was a successful confrontation of someone who had sin in his life because it brought David to the place of realizing his wrongs, and consequently returning to God. Most people we discipline publicly are those whose sins are seen externally, but the worst sinners are the ones nobody can see.

Am I saying we shouldn't confront sin in church? God forbid! We should by all means rebuke sin but we should always remember that we want the brother who has sinned not run away from the house of God, but to run to God help and healing. Sometimes, I believe the Holy Spirit may direct that some people's sins be rebuked publicly so that others may learn from their mistakes, but that should be done with great wisdom so that people's faith is not destroyed and that they don't lose their fellowship with God.

"As for those who are guilty and persist in sin, rebuke and admonish them in the presence of all, so that the rest may be warned and stand in wholesome awe and fear. I solemnly charge you in the presence of God and of Christ Jesus and of the chosen angels that you guard and keep (these rules) without personal prejudice or favor, doing nothing from partiality" (1 Tim 5:20-21 Amplified).

When pastors or when church leaders administer church discipline to an erring member, they should ensure that they don't do it punitively but restoratively, and without any personal prejudice or partiality; they should deal with everyone the same way. There should not be one rule for the poor member and another rule for the rich member. The treatment must be the same. We must always remember that God our Father, and Jesus Christ our Lord, and the elect angels are all watching how we treat and discipline church members.

No church member should be given preferential treatment at the expense of another. Some people have been hurt in church by this kind of attitude from some church leaders. It makes others feel embarrassed publicly right in church by the person or people who are supposed to lead them well, fairly and impartially together with the rest of the church members. A good leader must not show partiality in matters of church discipline. Standards of church discipline must be the same for all members. There are many pastors that are on record of giving preferential treatment to members that are rich at the expense of those that are economically challenged. Moreover, the unfortunate thing is when this is obvious to everyone around.

"My brethren, do not hold the faith of our Lord Jesus Christ, the Lord of glory, with partiality. For if there should come into your assembly a man with gold rings, in fine apparel, and there should also come in a poor man in filthy clothes, and you pay attention to the one wearing the fine clothes and say to him, 'You sit there in a good place,' and say to the poor man, 'You stand there,' or 'Sit here at my footstool,' Have you not shown partiality among yourselves, and become judges with evil

thoughts? Listen, my brethren: has God not chosen the poor of this world to be rich in faith and heirs of the kingdom which He promised to those who love Him? But you have dishonored the poor man. Do not the rich oppress you and drag you to courts? Do they not blaspheme that noble name by which you are called? If you really fulfil the royal law according to the Scripture, 'You shall love your neighbor as yourself,' you do well; but if you show partiality, you commit sin, and are convicted by the law as transgressors. For whoever shall keep the whole law and yet stumbles in one point, he is guilty of all" (James 2:1-10)

Church hurt from the pulpit is real, it is not new, it was there even in the early church and it is there in today's church.

Hurt in the Prophetic Church

Furthermore, it is painful to note that some families have been destroyed because of words and actions from the pulpit by words spoken to them as prophecies of words of knowledge. A certain visiting prophet called out a woman and gave her a prophetic word of knowledge, revealing that her husband was HIV positive and had extra marital affairs she didn't know about. The husband was not present in that church service as he was not a born-again Christian. The prophet went back to his town and left unresolved marital issues in that family. That marriage was dissolved and scattered. Was this the work of the Holy Spirit to destroy the family? I cannot comment or judge. All I know is that a family was broken like many others after a prophetic service.

You may have not experienced such kind of hurt before. But I must state that this kind of behavior is very common in the prophetic and deliverance churches. Many have been hurt from the pulpit as they have been told to be possessed with demons, being witches, wizards and agents of the devil due to various reasons. One thing that is common in the church that is predominantly prophetic or deliverance-oriented ministry is that if you disagree or have a different opinion on a particular issue, you will be easily named "possessed with an evil spirit". I have met a number of people whose commitment to God's house has been destroyed because they were called demonic, possessed and so on (this is not to say that all prophetic or deliverance-oriented churches are bad, but this is in keeping with the subject of discussion to help hurting people that have experienced church hurt).

I've seen well-meaning parents surrender their young people especially teens to undergo long deliverance sessions hoping to remove from them the evil spirit that makes them disobedient and problematic. However, I have no doubt in the fact that most unruly children are being controlled by evil spirits, especially if they have not yet given their lives to Lord Jesus Christ. But at the same time, I also understand that certain behaviors come as result of the type of parenting one receives, the child's background, peer pressure, teenage-hood, among other things. Such children whose upbringing is from a dysfunctional home or from broken Christian homes find themselves in church and we quickly rebel them demonic without fully understanding why they are behaving in such a manner. This even breaks them more and more. The place that should have given them healing breaks them even further. Most young people are not interested in anything to do with church because church called them demonic. When such people grow up, they end up resenting church forever and are very bitter against pastors.

Pulpit hurt varies in degrees. At one point as we attended church, we may have been hurt by one or two occurrences. We all need healing from it, starting from the preacher to the congregation. Don't run away from church, heal from church hurt.

CHAPTER**8**

RELIGIOUS ENSLAVEMENT

"For you put up with fools gladly, since you yourselves are wise! <u>For you put up with it if one brings you into bondage</u>, if one devours you, if one takes from you, if one exalts himself, if one strikes you on the face"

(2 Cor 11:19-20)

We have many people that come to church bound, oppressed and afflicted. Instead of them getting set free; we see their situation being made worse. Religious enslavement makes converts worse than they were before. People are in bondage while being part of the institution which is supposed to be a place where people come to be set free from various afflictions and bondages.

"Woe to you scribes and Pharisees, hypocrites! For you travel land and sea to win one proselyte, and when he is won, you make him twice as much a son of hell as yourselves" (Matt 23:15)

1. Legalism vs Liberty

Legalism is said to be a strict adherence to law over justice, mercy, grace and common sense.

Theologically, it is a doctrine of salvation by strictly adhering to the requirements of divine law. Legalism is about strict religious rules that make slaves of people.

When people are legalistic, their actions fall short of justice, mercy, grace and even common sense. Jesus denounced the Pharisees and scribes in His time for being meticulously strict about adherence to the law of tithing, yet neglecting the weightier matters of the Law, such as justice and mercy and faith. The former brings into religious bondage, while the latter brings into freedom.

"Woe to you, scribes and Pharisees, hypocrites! For you pay tithe of mint and anise and cummin, and have neglected the weightier of the law: justice and mercy and faith. These you ought to have done, without leaving the others undone. Blind guides, who strain out a gnat and swallow a camel"
(Matt 23:23-24).

Circumcision and observing the law was such a big issue in the early church, that it raised so much debate and controversy among the elect. Jewish believers wanted the gentile believers to also undergo circumcision and to observe the law, but the apostles, particularly Peter, James and Paul intervened to allow the believers to live in their new-found liberty in Christ. One does not become righteous and get saved on account of circumcision and observance of the law but on the basis of faith in Jesus Christ.

"And certain men came down from Judea and taught the brethren, 'Unless you are circumcised according to the custom of Moses, you cannot be saved. Therefore, when Paul and Barnabas had no small dissension and dispute with them, they determined that Paul and Barnabas and certain others of them should go up to Jerusalem, to the apostles and elders, about this question… Now the apostles and elders came together to consider this matter. And when there had been much disputing, Peter rose up and said to them, 'Men and brethren, you know that a good while ago God chose among us, that by my mouth the Gentiles should hear the word of the gospel and believe. So God, who knows the heart,

acknowledged them by giving the Holy Spirit, just as He did to us. And made no distinction between us and them, purifying their hearts by faith. Now therefore, why do you test God by putting a yoke on the neck of the disciples which neither our fathers nor we are able to bear? But we believe that through the grace of the Lord Jesus Christ, we shall be saved in the same manner as they" (Acts 15:1,2,6-11).

The debates and controversies in the early church did not end with this Jerusalem council. It continued in several other churches where legalistic Jewish believers and teachers advanced their legalistic beliefs and customs among the brethren. At every point the apostles had to intervene and bring order.

Paul wrote to the church at Galatia rebuking them for having begun in the spirit, following the right way of grace but they were back and now stuck in the flesh in trying to live by the law. He further instructed them to stand firm in their new-found freedom in Christ and not be entangled again with the yoke of the bondage of religiosity.

*"**Stand fast therefore in the liberty by which Christ has made us free, and do not be entangled again with a yoke of bondage**. Indeed, Paul, say to you that if you become circumcised, Christ will profit you nothing…You have become estranged from Christ, you who attempt to be justified by law; you have fallen from grace…You ran well. Who hindered you from obeying the truth?... For you brethren, **have been called to liberty**; only do not use your liberty as an opportunity for the flesh, but through love serve one another"* (Gal 5:1-7,13).

Legalistic leaders and teachers abuse and stretch God's word by making strict rules out of it for the people to adhere to them, and consequently making the slaves. These are leaders that make strict rules such as the "dos and don'ts" to make people feel incomplete without those rules and traditions. In the legalistic tendencies bring bondage and eventually hurt.

"Beware, lest anyone cheat you through philosophy and empty deceit, according to the traditions of men, according to the basic principles of this world, and not according to Christ... Therefore, if you died with Christ from the basic principles of this world, why. As though living in the world, do you subject yourself to regulations – do not touch, do not taste, do not handle, which all concern things which perish with the using – according to the commandments and doctrines of men? These things indeed have an appearance of wisdom in self-imposed religion, false humility, and neglect of the body, but are of no value against the indulgence of the flesh" (Col 2:8,20-23)

Fasting is a good Christian devotion but there are some very legalistic leaders that have enslaved people by making them go through crude periods of fasting, to the point of even having them neglect their physical health, supposing that by so doing. They are bringing their flesh under control and becoming more spiritual as it were. Due to this kind of religious enslavement, we have heard of some people who have died during fasting, and some have weakened their immunity and become sick.

Some legalistic rules have to do with strict devotion to prayer meetings, church services, giving of offerings that are done in an extreme and abusive manner. In such churches systems where legalism is the order and modus operandi, nobody is allowed to suggest otherwise, but rather do as commanded. Those who bring up other ideas and suggestions are labeled rebellious. Everything the leader speaks becomes law in such churches. There is no liberty in such places. Where there is no liberty, people are oppressed, abused and hurt.

2. Control and Manipulation

Another form of religious enslavement in church today is control and manipulation of people through superstition. Superstition is religion based on some mystical power rather than reason or God's power. Superstition is a kind of fear driven religion. If at all you are fear motivated to practice any religious devotion, then you are in bondage. Fear brings bondage and torment. There is no love in fear. The Christian faith is meant to be love driven and not fear driven. God doesn't force anyone to worship and serve Him. We don't serve God out of fear. Our love for God should be a response to His love which He already has for us.

"For you did not receive the spirit of bondage again to fear, but you received the Spirit of Adoption by whom we cry out, 'Abba, Father.' The Spirit Himself bears witness with our spirit that we are children of God" (Rom 8:15-16).

"Love has been perfected among us in this: that we may have boldness in the day of Judgment; because as He is, so are we in this world. There is no fear in love; but perfect love casts away fear, because fear involves torment. But he who fears has not been made perfect in love. We love because He first loved us" (1 John 4:17-19).

The law brought fear and bondage. Many obeyed the law out of fear of punishment, and that was bondage in itself. We being in Christ should no longer serve God out of fear but love.

There are religious leaders today in the church that lead people by instilling fear in them in order to control them. Some people are told whenever they want to marry, travel, do business or do anything that they have to tell their leader first and he must approve of it or they won't have to do it. He must approve and determine where you must go and what you must do, even with personal matters. These are cultic tendencies. This particular behavior is a form of emotional manipulation.

One lady I met told me that she belonged to one church where she felt so hurt because of the actions of the pastor and was willing to leave, but that the pastor had told her that curses, bad things and misfortunes awaited her if she left the church. I told her that she was being manipulated and that she needed to leave with immediate effect. I advised her not allow herself to be a victim of intimidation and vain threats. I assured her that nothing bad would happen to her if she left.

In some churches, especially some prophetic churches fear is the drive. People receive prophesies of misfortune, death, and other bad things and are instructed to give certain things to avert the impending things mentioned.

Control and manipulation are some of the devil's great weapons. Control and manipulation are actually a form of witchcraft. Paul wrote to the Galatian church and said to them that by trying to keep the law to maintain their salvation, they were acting out of the fear and manipulation instilled in them by legalistic teachers.

"O foolish Galatians! Who has bewitched you that you should not obey the truth, before whose eyes Jesus Christ was portrayed among you as crucified? This only I want to learn from you: Did you receive the Spirit by the works of the law, or by the hearing of faith? Are you so foolish? Having began in the Spirit, are you now being made perfect by the flesh? (Gal 3:1-3)

Paul actually called the people in the Galatian church foolish, for allowing themselves to be brought into bondage like that. He also wrote to the Corinthian church to rebuke them for having allowed themselves to be fooled by fools, "the super-apostles" who they received and put up with their shenanigans.

"For you put up with fools gladly, since you yourselves are wise! For you put up with it if one brings you into bondage..." (2 Cor 11:19-20).

Some leaders are so hypocritical. They keep away the key of knowledge from the people so that they control them. Withholding keys represents control. People are not told the whole of God's liberating truth. The knowledge of truth that could make people free is withheld in order to keep them in bondage and to perpetuate their suffering, and to always make the people to depend on them.

"Woe to you lawyers! For you have taken away the key of knowledge. You did not enter in yourselves, and those who were entering in you hindered" (Luke 11:52)

"Then Jesus said to those who believed Him, 'If you abide in My word, you are My disciples indeed. And you shall know the truth, and the truth shall make you free" (John 8:31-32)

Religious enslavement has a way of manipulating and controlling even the educated. To be free of religious enslavement, church folk should decide now to go into church with their minds without leavingthem outside. People must now be like the believers at Berea, who are said to have been so noble. For each time they left church service, they went home, and read and searched the scriptures for themselves to see whether what was taught at church was agreeing with the Scriptures. Know the Scriptures for yourself and for your own liberty.

"Then the brethren immediately sent Paul and Silas away by night to Berea. When they arrived, they went into the Synagogue of the Jews. These were more fair-minded than those in Thessalonica, in that they received the word with all readiness, and searched the scriptures daily to find out whether these things were so. Therefore, many of them believed, and also not a few of the Greeks, prominent women as well as men" (Acts 17:10-12)

3. Exploitation

"You put up with it when someone enslaves you, takes everything you have, takes advantage of you..." (2 Cor 11:20 NLT)

Believers are being exploited by the ministers whose aim is to enslave them and exploit them for their money and material possessions. In order to advance their agenda, such ministers abuse the word of God, by twisting it and adulterating it.

"For we are not, like many, (like hucksters making a trade of) peddling God's word (short-changing and adulterating the divine message); but like men of sincerity and the purest motive, as commissioned and sent by God, we speak His message in Christ (the Messiah), in the very sight and presence of God" (2 Cor 2:17 Amplified)

"In their greed they will make up clever lies to get hold of your money..." (2 Pet 2:3a NLT)

You could be one of the many people today that have suffered exploitation under these shrewd hypocritical ministers. Unfortunately, their victims are not only rich but widows also, especially those going through various problems in life.

"Woe to you, scribes and Pharisees, hypocrites! ***For you devour widows' houses, and for a pretense make long prayers.*** *Therefore, you will receive greater condemnation"* (Matt 23:14)

Sadly, we have people who use others only as tools to make money in church. Church attendance is money driven. When the leader sees people gathered, he sees money and how he will exploit them of their money, and not ministering to their entire being.

4. Abuse and Shame

Time and again we continue to see and hear reports of how people have been abused and publicly shamed in the church.

"You put up with it when someone enslaves you, takes everything you have, ***takes advantage of you,***

*takes control of everything, and **slaps you in the face**"* (2 Cor 11:20).

Some women are sexually abused, taking advantage of their vulnerabilities and weaknesses. People in churches where such abuse happen are cultured in such a way that they protect their abusive leader at all costs in the name of "covering your father's nakedness". Leaders in such churches are held in the high esteem of nigh moral perfection, and people cannot say a word about any misdemeanor of any kind that the leader may have done. The common scripture to shut them up is always, *"Touch not my anointed…"* (Ps 105:15).

"They are a kind who work their way into people's homes and win the confidence of vulnerable women who are burdened with the guilt of sin and controlled by various desires. Such women are forever following new teachings, but they are never able to understand the truth" (2 Tim 3:6-7)

This is so typical of some parts of today's church. Vulnerable women that are being taken advantage of and abused are all over. Because of their vulnerability (emotional or social-economic vulnerability), their spiritual weakness and their state of being devoid of the knowledge of the truth, they are even more vulnerable to religious and sexual abuse.

5. Entitlement Mentality

Religious enslavement is by and large advanced by leaders that have an entitlement mentality.These are leaders who are obsessed with fame and a sense of entitlement. These leaders want to take control of everything and everyone around them, if possible, even the very sensitive private and personal matters of their followers. These are leaders that are extremely domineering.

"But all their works they do to be seen by men. They make their phylacteries broad and enlarge the borders of their garments. They love the best places at feasts, the best seats in the synagogues, greetings in the marketplaces, and to be called 'Rabbi, Rabbi'; for One is your Teacher, the Christ, and you all are brethren. Do not call anyone on earth your father; for One is your Father, He who is in heaven. And do not be called teachers; for One is your Teacher, the Christ. But he who is greatest among you shall be your servant. And whoever exalts himself will be

humbled, and he who humbles himself will be exalted" (Matt 23:5-12).

The indication here is that no one and no leader should take the place of Christ and God in our lives. Leaders should never be venerated and exalted to such a position that Christ becomes second to the people they lead.

A leader must not be domineering, but to lead by example *"Not domineering (as arrogant, dictatorial and over-bearing persons) over those in your charge, but being examples (patterns and models of Christian living) to the flock (the congregation)"* (1 Pet 5:3 Amplified).

A leader must not be preoccupied and obsessed with pre-eminence, position and entitlement. Such leaders bring so much hurt not only on the members of the church but also on the mission of the church. Apostle John wrote to the church at Ephesus and warned of Diotrephes, a very domineering controlling leader that was so obsessed with entitlement and position the he would not welcome the apostle John himself or any other missionaries. He even went further to use malicious words against them and forbade the members of the church from receiving anybody without his approval or they would suffer the punishment of being ex-communicated from the church.

"I wrote to the church, but Diotrephes, who loves to have the pre-eminence among them, does not receive us. Therefore, if I come, I will call to mind his deeds which he does, prating against us with malicious words. And not content with that, he himself does not receive the brethren, and forbids those who wish to, putting them out of the church" (3 John 9-10).

Diotrephes kind of a leader is one who treats the church like he owns it, and one who loves to control people and is actually not so kind and hospitable to anybody. Diotrephes overstretched his jurisdiction to the point that he was even in control of the homes of the members of the Ephesian church. He needed to approve who they needed to welcome in their homes. He instructed who goes and who stays. What gave him that audacity? An entitlement mentality. That obviously brought so much hurt in that church. Domineering leaders are very hurtful.

Examples of Pastors with Extreme Entitlement Mentality

- There are pastors who do not allow their followers to make any movements until they approve it as their pastor.For example, to visit a family, to go on holiday, make abusiness or work trips among other things.

- There are pastors who do not allow their followers to start a relationship until they approve it as their pastor.

- There are pastors who do not allow their followers to have sex with their wives or husbands until their pastor approves.

- There are pastors who teach women submission first to the pastor then later to the husband.

- There are pastors who possess personal properties of members such as cars, houses, cell phones and other valuables as belonging to them because they are their pastor.

- Some pastors feel entitled to all church finances. They take all the tithes, offerings and seeds given by the members and leave the church coffers empty.

- When some pastors pray for someone and they have a financial breakthrough or get a job, promotion, they feel entitled to receive an amount of money from them monthly.

- Some pastors have a habit of abruptly barging in on their members' privacy unannounced and uninvited. Though it may be seen as pastoral care and visitation but it's an entitlement mentality when done in extremes.

Examples of Church Members with Extreme Entitlement Mentality

- They want their pastor to stop everything he is doing and attend to them when they want his attention.
- They feel entitled to their pastor's personal property as belongs to them also. They want to drive his car, live in his house, wear his clothes.
- They don't believe their pastor needs his privacy. They visit his house without invitation, walk around hisrooms, open his fridge and eat whatever they find without permission.
- They feel they can call and text their pastor anytime even when it's not an emergency. The pastor has to pick up each and every call they make and reply to every text message.

- They feel entitled to their pastor's money to sort out their financial difficulties. He must pay their rent, school fees, buy them food and other things. His money is theirs also.
- They feel entitled to attend their pastor's private functions such a birthday parties, weddings, graduations even without invitation.
- Some church members feel entitled to church finances. The church must take care of them, dress them, sponsor them, feed them, do everything for them even if they are not employed by the church.

Please understand this chapter in correct perspective. Yes, It is important to honor and hold in high esteem the man or woman of God you are under. It is important that you communicate with them and share your issues, movements and decisions for counsel and covering. What is not okay is when you are doing it out of fear and enslavement. That's not okay. It's a toxic entitlement mentality. What's not okay is to have a toxic religious entitlement.

6. Tolerance for religious enslavement

Paul rebuked the church at Corinth for having tolerated to be religiously enslaved by "super apostles", deceivers and leaders that wanted to take control of everything in their lives. Religious enslavement is responsible for so much hurt in the church today. But we have a choice not to put up with it. Paul's words to the church are so empowering. Nobody can be free from religious enslavement without taking a firm bold stand against it.

"For you put up with fools gladly, since you yourselves are wise! For you put up with it if one brings you into bondage, if one devours you, if one takes from you, if one exalts himself, if one strikes you on the face" (2 Cor 11:19-20)

CHAPTER 9

MORAL FAILURE

"It is actually reported that there is sexual immorality among you, and such sexual immorality as is not even named among the Gentiles – that a man has his father's wife!" (1 Cor 5:1)

As alluded to earlier, when we come to church, we have an expectation that all is now perfect since we have started this new journey with Christ who has washed us from all our sins. We have in our minds that church will be completely opposite from the world we are coming from. The expectation for moral excellence is very high. But, alas, we get the shock of our lives when we discover that the people in the church are also practicing the same sins we were practicing before we surrendered to Christ.

A common reason why a lot of people have given up on church is because of hypocrisy. Christians say one thing but do the direct opposite. This sad reality has broken so many people, and you may just be one of them. It is unfortunate that this sad reality is traceable to the men and women on the pulpit. This has made many people to just return back to the ways of the world because they see no difference in lifestyle between the church and the world they are coming from.

1. Immorality in Church

The sexual immorality that exits among Christians is something that is devastating. It's as though one cannot belong to church for a year without hearing a story of someone who is involved in ungodly sexual activities. Sometimes it's stories about the main pastor or the priest sleeping with female members of the church, or assistant pastors having sexual affairs. Elders and deacons also find themselves involved in ungodly sexual activities in today's church.

I know of a lady who had given her life to Christ and was then delivered from prostitution. She joined a particular church where she was later introduced to the senior prophet of the ministry who was married. Before long, they were in a sexual relationship and she became pregnant. From the last time I saw her, she has since returned to the world and does not believe anything you tell her about church. The worst part is that many people got to know of the immoral secret lifestyle of the man of God and it discouraged their commitment to the faith and to the church.

Hearing that your pastor or church leader is involved in illicit sexual affairs with fellow church members can be heart breaking. This is another form of church that most people go through when they come to church. The people who are supposed to teach them the word are the ones involved in ungodly acts. How then can one continue to sit and listen to them preach the Word of God?

"You therefore, who teach another, do you not teach yourself? You who preach that man should not steal, do you steal? You who say, 'Do not commit adultery,' do you commit adultery? You who abhor idols, do you rob temples? You who make your boast in the law, do you dishonor God through breaking the law? For 'the name of God is blasphemed among the Gentiles because of you,' as it is written" (Rom 2:21-24)

Sexual affairs among church members who are not married to each other are a common phenomenon in churches today. This has hurt a lot of new converts. Once they join church, they become targets for sex among the brethren. Scandals of abortions and unwanted pregnancies have become a norm among us. This a sad constant occurrence that has saddened many people and broken the hearts of so many parents who sent their children to church hoping that their children will be transformed but only to be told that their child lost their virginity to a church boy. Instead of getting healed at church, People have gotten HIV and other STIs from church. Young people are losing their virginity to fellow church folk. Rape cases are happening among church brethren.

Pastors and church leaders are being sued for rape. Bisexual relationships are common among Christians even when the Bible does not approve of such abominations.

Many people are hurting because some fellow church member defrauded or cheated them by violating their marriage through infidelity with the spouse.

God's will is for you to be holy; so stay away from all sexual sin. Then each of you will control his own body and live in holiness and honor – not in lustful passion like the pagans who do not know God and His ways. Never harm or cheat a fellow believer in this matter by violating his wife; for the Lord avenges such sins as we have solemnly warned you before. God has called us to live holy lives, not impure lives. Therefore, anyone who refuses to live by these rules is not disobeying human teaching but is rejecting God, who gives His Holy Spirit to you"

(1 Thess 4:3-8 NLT)

One such example is the man who was having a sexual relationship with his father's wife and that obviously not only hurt his father but many people in the church at Corinth. Paul had to intervene in the matter to excommunicate the brother from fellowship. Fortunately, in this case the man repented, was forgiven by the church members and restored in the fellowship. Adultery happening among church fellow members brings a lot of hurt.

"It is actually reported that there is sexual immorality among you, and such sexual immorality as is not even named among the Gentiles – that a man has his father's wife!" (1 Cor 5:1)

"I am not overstating it when I say that the man who caused all the trouble hurt all of you more than he hurt me. Most of you opposed him, and that was punishment enough. Now however, it is time to forgive and comfort him. Otherwise he may be overcome by discouragement. So I urge you now to reaffirm your love for him. I wrote to you as I did not test you and see if you would fully comply with my instructions. When you forgive this man, I forgive him, too. And when I forgive whatever needs to be forgiven, I do so with Christ's authority for your benefit, so that Stan

will not outsmart us. For we are familiar with his evil schemes"

(2 Cor 2:5-11 NLT)

We read of the Old Testament story of David and how he abused his power by defrauding his subject and soldier in his army. Uriah, was an upright man. David violated his wife Bathsheba at the time the man had gone to the battlefield, and later on got him killed on the battlefield. Where there is sexual sin, be rest assured that other sins will follow.

The extent at which sexual sins have infiltrated the church has caused many families and individuals to be so hurt that they don't want anything to do with the church again.

Two Kinds of Immoral Pastors

Here the two kinds of sexually immoral pastors in reference to their sexual and moral conduct:

(a) The Carnal Pastor

- He does not fornicate for any diabolic reason or fulfill any evil covenant. He simply fornicates because he is a carnally minded pastor.

- The carnal pastor has a sexual weakness which he cannot control. When he sees an attractive lady in his congregation, he wants to sleep with her to satisfy his lustful desires.

- The carnal pastor is genuinely called and may flow and operate perfectly well in his spiritual gifts but is struggling with sexual immorality.

- The carnal pastor is often remorseful after falling into a sexual sin. He often vows never to do it again but again finds himself in the same sin.

- The carnal pastor usually does not have a mentor. If he does, he doesn't sincerely discuss his moral failures and weaknesses with his mentor. Either he is not open enough to seek the needed help from his mentor or he doesn't listen to his mentor's advice on moral issues.

a) The Diabolic Pastor

- The diabolic pastor indulges in sexual activities mainly in order to fulfill an evil covenant.

- The diabolic pastor is an occultist, a ritualist and possibly involved in satanism or witchcraft.

- He may not necessarily want to involve in multiple sex activities but is forced to do so because that's what is required of him from the evil altars.

- The diabolic pastor uses evil powers to lure women into sleeping with him. Many ladies do not understand how they found themselves sleeping with their pastor.

- The diabolic pastor has no regret or guilt for any sexual sins he commits with his fellow members. His conscience is seared.

- The diabolic pastor usually has a diabolic mentor who initiates him into evil dealings.

- The diabolic pastor may not be as gifted, but uses diabolic powers to operate in the supernatural, hence the sexual activity is one of the requirements for fulfilling diabolical rituals.

2. Financial Mismanagement

Another area that has contributed to a lot of people getting terribly hurt in church is how finances of the church are handled and managed. Financial mismanagement or misappropriation in the church has been one area that has hurt many. Many people who genuinely gave to the work of God, but never saw the money being used for its intended purpose have ended up greatly disappointed and discouraged to engage themselves in supporting the work of the ministry financially.

It's sad to mention that some church leaders have been overtaken by greed and have rather used all church funds for their personal gains. I have discovered that people who stopped giving to the church have been hurt by the fact that at some point they gave for particular cause in the house of God, and their contributions were either misappropriated or mismanaged.

In the recent past we have seen our anointed men and women of God being unfaithful in the handling of kingdom finances. It is sad to see men of God who are supposed to be God's mouth piece getting arrested for money laundering and fraud cases. This has been one of the greatest reasons why many people have stayed away from the church. One of the ethics of Christian leadership is that a Christian leader must be above reproach, even in relation to finances:

*"This is a faithful saying: if a man desires the position of a bishop, he desires a good work. A bishop then must be blameless; the husband of one wife, temperate, sober-minded, of good behavior, hospitable, able to teach; not given to wine, not violent, **not greedy for money**, but gentle, not quarrelsome, **not covetous"***

(1 Tim 3:1-3)

*"Shepherd the flock of God which is among you, serving as overseers, not by compulsion but willingly, **not for dishonest gain but eagerly**; nor as being lords over those entrusted to you, but being examples to the flock; and when the Chief Shepherd appears, you will receive the crown of glory that does not fade away"*

(1 Pet 5:2-4)

I believe in prosperity because *"silver and gold is mine"* saith the Lord(Haggai 2:8). I also believe that every person especially Christians must prosper financially in order to live a good and honorable life, taking care of themselves, their families and dependents.

"Beloved, I pray that you may prosper in all things and be in health, just as your soul prospers" (3 John 2)

I strongly believe that it is from a genuine heart to see people prosper that a good pastor wants to see his members break out of financial frustrations and struggles hence the introductions of business ideas, business seminars and other initiatives in the church. I honestly have no problem with these ideas only that business in church has been a major source of church hurt.

Pastors and church leaders and Christians have been at the center of heavy business failures, money scheme failure and village banking failure in local churches. Because people's monies are involved, many have left church. Sometimes the pastor may not even be involved but the members among themselves have so many issues against one another relating to the business initiatives they embarked in that failed.

Christian business partners operate with mediocrity simply because they attend the same church. They will not offer excellent services for whatever reason and this breaks down relationships among believers. You will always hear poor service delivery, late payments, excuses upon excuses every time church people are doing business among themselves. They will always want to get products and services at a way cheaper price simply because you attend the same church. We hear of church members dragging each other to court because of the hurt experienced as a result of financial fraud among themselves. Such were even the happenings that characterized the Corinthian church and we see that even in today's church. This conduct brings the name of the church into disrepute and maligns the gospel of our Lord Jesus Christ.

"When one of you has a dispute with another believer, how dare you file a lawsuit and ask a secular court to decide the matter instead of taking it to other believers... if you have legal disputes about such matters, why go to outside judges who are not respected by the church? I am saying this to shame you. isn't there anyone in all the church who is wise enough to decide these issues? But instead, one believer sues another – right in front of unbelievers. Even to have such lawsuits with one another is a defeat for you. why not just accept the injustice and leave it at that? Why not let yourself be cheated? Instead, you yourselves are

the ones who do wrong and cheat even your fellow believers" (1 Cor 6:1,4-8 NLT)

We are quick to point out corruption in the political circles, especially among government officials, but we have failed to judge and deal with the corruption happening inside the church. Corruption is said to be an abuse of power, and rightly so.We have seen how people in church have abused their power and positions of authority to defraud fellow believers of their finances. We have church leaders defrauding the church by embezzling church monies. To use the terms "mismanagement or misappropriation of church finances" even sounds so polite, when the misconduct is done by someone who is supposed to lead the flock of God on a right path. It should be referred to as Church Corruption.

3. Compromise of Character

Effective leadership has two hands – character and competence. A leader must have skill (competence), but must also have integrity (character). A leader must be professional. Every profession has its own ethics. A leader cannot expect to effectively discharge his duties if he or she compromises on either or both of the said hands. Some leaders are so gifted and skilled but they compromise on the ethics of leadership, and that makes them to fail as leaders and to fail the people they have been entrusted to lead. Some people are competent but their corrupt tendencies make them unprofessional on the job.

Competence must go hand in hand with character. Skillfulness must go together with integrity. I know of people that are so gifted and skilled – they are so competent, but they have no character, they have no integrity.

As alluded to earlier, David is said to have been chosen by God to lead His people, and he led them through the integrity of his heart (character) and guided them by the skillfulness of his hands (competence)

*"He also chose David His servant, and took him from the sheepfold; from following the ewes that had young he brought him, to shepherd Jacob His people, and Israel His inheritance. So he shepherded them according to the **integrity of his heart**, and guided them by the **skillfulness ofhis hands**"*(Psalm 78:70-72).

David had a good testimony of leadership, but when he compromised on his character, it cost him a great deal in life and leadership. He abused his power by committing adultery with the wife of one of his faithful subjects.

Compromise on your character will make you lose your moral standing (birthright, Christian heritage), and consequently cause you to miss on certain favors and blessings of God. Esau is said to be a man that was a skillful hunter but a very compromising man. He had an ungodly character, a weak will and a poor bargaining ability, and that cost him his birthright and eventually the blessings attached to it. He compromised on his birthright for his appetite. Esau also compromised morally by his sexual misdemeanor. Esau was polygamous and married heathen women that brought so much hurt and pain to his parents.

*"Pursue peace with all people, and holiness, without which no one will see the Lord**... lest there be any fornicator or profane person like Esau, who for one morsel of food sold his birthright**. For you know that afterward, when he wanted to inherit the blessing, he was rejected, for he found no place for repentance, though he sought it diligently with tears"* (Hebrews 12:14,16,17)

*"So the boys grew. And Esau was **a skillful hunter**, a man of the field; but Jacob was a mild man, dwelling in tents… And Jacob cooked a stew, and Esau came in from the field, and he was weary. And Esau said to Jacob, 'Please feed me with that same red stew, for I am weary.' Therefore, his name was called Edom. But Jacob said, 'Sell me your birthright as of this day.' And Esau said, 'Look, I am about to die; so what is this birthright to me?' Then Jacob said, 'Swear to me as of this day.' So he swore to him, and sold his birthright to Jacob. And Jacob gave Esau bread and stew of lentils; then he ate and drank, arose and went his way. Thus Esau despised his birthright"* (Gen 25:27,29-34)

*"When Esau was forty years old, he took as wives Judith the daughter of Beeri the Hittite, and Basemath the daughter of Elon the Hittite. **And thy were a grief of mind to Isaac and Rebekah**"* (Gen 26:34)

Each and every one of us must learn to muzzle our appetites and to lead ourselves first, especially for those of us who are in positions of leadership. Ungodly appetites bring shame on one's life and leadership. Because of his untamed appetite, Esau upon having traded his birthright for a bowl of red soap was even nicknamed Edom, which meant Red. Today, some leaders in the church and the church itself are called names and the world is making fun of them because of character compromise. The church is being maligned and defamed on account of the immoral conduct of its leaders and people that follow their immoral ways.

"And many will follow their immoral ways and lasciviousness; because of them the true Way will be maligned and defamed" (2 Pet 2:2 Amplified).

CHAPTER**10**

UNDERSTANDING THE CHURCH SOCIETY

"For it has been declared to me concerning you, my brethren, by those of Chloe's household, that there are contentions among you" (1 Cor 1:11)

"What is causing the quarrels and fights among you? Don't they come from the evil desires at war within you?" (James 4:1)

The Ideal Church

The ideal church should have unity, peace, joy, impartiality, hospitality, patience, respect, kindness and love, purity and holiness, integrity and seriousness, and a gossip-free environment among its members. The ideal church should be without spot or wrinkle.

"Husbands, love your wives, just as Christ also loved the church and gave Himself for her, that He might sanctify and cleanse her with the washing of water by the word, that He might present her to Himself a glorious church, not having spot or wrinkle or any such thing, but that she should be holy and without blemish"

(Eph 5:2-7)

The Mixed Multitude

However, the reality is that we have an imperfect church and until Jesus Christ comes back, we will continue to have an imperfect, spotted and wrinkled church. We have a church with different kinds of members with various behaviors and attitudes both positive and negative.

- We have people who bring positive energy, yet also others who bring negative energy in the fellowship.

- We have loving and kind people, as well as those who are unloving and unkind.
- We have those who spread the gospel, as well as those who spread the gossip.
- We have those who are very unifying, and we also have those who nullify unity among the brethren.
- We have peace-seekers and peace-makers, and we also have peace breakers.
- We have those who have integrity and seriousness, as well as those who don't.
- We have those who value purity and holiness, as well as those who are immoral.
- We have leaders who lead by good example with humility, as well as those who are abusive, domineering and proud.
- We have people who come hurting, and we also have those who actually cause and perpetuate hurt on others.
- We have the rich and we have the poor.
- We have the old and we have the young.
- We have men and we have women.
- We have children, young adults and old adults.
- We have the married and we have the single and the divorced.

- We have the healthy and we have the sick.
- We have those who come with all kinds of problems and bondages, and we also have those who cause more oppression and bondage on others.
- We have the forgiving as well as the unforgiving.
- We have those who are jealous
- We have those who bring strife and confusion.
- We have very confident and courageous people, as well as those who are fearful.
- We have the strong as well as the weak.
- We have those who come with all kinds of mental problems, as well as those who actually cause mental problems to others within thc church.
- We even have those who want to get those suffering from mental illness healed.
- We have drug, alcohol and even sex addicts coming to church.
- We have people with sobriety, as well as those with toxic behaviors.
- We havethose who stand for the truth and advance the truth.

- We also have those who don't, but spread falsehood and lies.
- We have the zealous, as well as the lukewarm.
- We have the educated and the uneducated.
- We have those who stand for impartiality, as well as those who advance partiality in the church.
- We have those who quarrel.
- We have the selfless, as well as the selfish.
- We have those who are honest as well as those who are dishonest.
- We have those who borrow money then return and those who won't return.
- We even have thieves in the church society.
- We have confessors of good, as well as complainers, murmurers and grumblers.
- We have those who live in their freedom in Christ, as well as those who are bound in legalism.
- We have those who are truthful and real, but we also have those who pretend.

*"Now the **mixed multitude** who were among them yielded to intense craving; **so the children of Israel also wept again and said:** 'Who will give us meat to Eat? We remember the fish which we ate*

freely in Egypt, the cucumbers, the melons, the leeks, the onions, and the garlic, but now our whole being is dried up; there is nothing at all except this manna before our eyes!" (Num 11:7-9).

"Then the **foreign rabble** *who were traveling with the Israelites began to crave the things of Egypt.*
And the people of Israel also began to complain.
'Oh for some meat! They exclaimed" (Num 11:4 NLT).

The New Living Translation of the Bible calls the mixed multitude as the **"foreign rabble"** who were traveling with the Israelites that began to crave the good things of Egypt and influenced the whole congregation of the Israelites to do the same - to murmur and complain against God. There are people in church who are a foreign rabble, influencing everybody to be discontented and to have a craving for the things of the world. Everyone coming to church should be aware of the mixed multitude they will find

The term **"rabble"** or **"to rabble",** means to speak in a confused manner, to talk incoherently; to utter nonsense.In the church society you will find those who speak in a confused manner, talk incoherently, and utter nonsense. Such people are strange and they bring so much confusion, discontent, strife, divisions and hurt in the church. They are a mixed multitude that wield so much negative energy and influence, and tend to plant discontent and confusion among the church members. They are agents of the spirit of confusion which is the major source of church hurt.

With all the rabble, the imperfections, the spots, the negative energy, the gossip, the quarrels, the hate, the bitterness, the love for money and pleasure as opposed to love for God, the selfishness, the arrogance, the confusion, the divisions, the strife, the jealousy, the impatience, the cruelty, the abuse, the exploitation, the immorality, the corruption and fraud, the falsehood and lies, and many more evils that people come with into church as well as find in church, it should not surprise anyone that we have church hurt.

Some people serving in church have issues and hurts of their own, and they get to transfer that onto others within the church as a way of dealing with their already exiting pains. How many of us can be honest enough to admit that we actually went to church with an attitude and some negative energy and we ended up causing hurt to others?

We all go to church with different moods. We sometimes go to church after having had a bad day or a bad week making us go in grumpy. Sometimes we go to church after having had a very difficult period and the only way to deal with their problems is to vent orlash it out on others, thus hurting many innocent people at church.

A Society with Apostates

In the church society, you will find apostates (people who have backslidden and renounced their Christian faith but continue to attend church) both members and leaders alike. These people have caused so much confusion, divisions and church hurt.

"In the same way, these people who claim authority from their dreams – live immoral lives… When these people eat with you in your fellowship meals commemorating the Lord's love, they are dangerous reefs that can shipwreck you… They told you that in the last times there would be scoffers whose purpose in life is to satisfy their ungodly desires. These people are the ones who are creating divisions among you" (Jude 8,12,18,19 NLT)

The reality is that the people in the church society come from the worldly society, and even if you were to leave for the world because of having been hurt in church, you will still find more hurtful people there. Understanding and preparing your mind about the people that you find in church, andlearning how you can live and deal with them will help minimize church hurt in your life.

Noah's ark is a perfect picture of the church. It contained different kinds of animals but they were all safe and secured in the ark. Some animals were harmful, poisonous and deadly yet they lived together in the ark without killing each other for the period. They learnt how to live together. You have to understand that when you come to church, you will not only find the good people. You will also find the bad characters. You will find those who are the exact representation of the world they are coming from. It should not be a surprise to you. Don't run away from church. Heal from church hurt.

CHAPTER 11

CHURCH HURT AND MENTAL HEALTH

"And as they were eating, He said, Solemnly I say to you, <u>one of you will betray Me</u>! They were exceedingly pained and distressed and deeply hurt and sorrowful and began to say to Him one after another, surely it cannot be I, Lord, can it?... Then Jesus went with them to a place called Gethsemane and He told His disciples, 'Sit down here while I go over yonder and pray.' And taking with Him Peter and the two sons of Zebedee, <u>He began to show grief and distress of mind and was deeply depressed. Then He said to them, My soul is very sad and deeply grieved, so that I am almost dying of sorrow</u>. Stay here and keep awake and keep watch with Me"

(Matt 26:21,22,36-38 Amplified)

In this chapter, I will be discussing a few things about mental health. I write this chapter with so much caution and carefulness knowing it's one of the most sensitive topics to touch on. The purpose of this chapter is not to discriminate nor condemn people going through mental health issues but to rather bring you a good understanding of what they are really going through.

Mental health refers to the well-being of a person's mind and emotional life. It is the ability for someone to deal with the inner space of thinking, feeling and managing life; the ability to start, develop and even sustain mutually fulfilling relationships. Even more, it is the ability for a person to sustain a spiritual life.

When you are mentally health you will have a sense of value for yourself and for others. When you are mentally health, you will be able to deal with your thoughts and feelings. When you are mentally health you will manage your life well. When you are mentally health you will initiate, develop and sustain mutually satisfying relationships more effectively, and you will be more effective in sustaining your spiritual life.

Therefore, people who are mentally health live their lives in such a way that they express a sense of self-esteem and strength to cope with whatever and whoever they face. They express values of self-care, relationships with family members, friends, those they work and interact with more often, utilizing their time, money, and even themselves efficiently. They also effectively take part in community activities and social events.

Now, people who suffer from mental illnesses experience the opposite of the values earlier mentioned. They tend to have low self-worth; they don't value other people. They tend to be weak in coping with life's situations; they have a problem to use time and money more effectively. They have problems dealing with their thoughts, feelings and to manage their lives more effectively. They have problems to initiate, develop and sustain mutually fulfilling relationships and to sustain their spiritual lives. When a person is not in the right frame of mind, the risks to make irrational decisions are very high, and this can lead to developing other mental disorders.

Mental Illness

This refers to a group of mental illnesses and disorders that greatly impact on a person's thoughts, perceptions, feelings, beliefs and behaviors. Mental illnesses are health conditions involving changes in emotion, thinking or behavior (or a combination of these). Mental illnesses are associated with distress and/or problems functioning in social, work or family activities (Parekh: 2018).

Mental illnesses cause disturbances in one's concentration, focus, and mood. The following behaviors may be associated with mental illness: depression, anxiety disorders, schizophrenia, eating disorders and addictive behaviors (Mayo Clinic: 2019). Mental illnesses have contributed to church hurt and destroyed many Christian relationships. Abuse of alcohol, drugs and extreme compulsiveness to sex are mostly examples of mental illnesses.

Mental illness indeed affects a person's thinking, perceptions, mood or behavior. Mental illness can make it difficult for someone to cope with work and church relationships. Church work can be demanding, engaging and stressful. Therefore, mental illnesses are issues we cannot afford to ignore. Church hurt can worsen and trigger mental illness.

Mental Disorders

Medline Plus gives the following definition of mental disorders: "mental disorders are conditions that affect your thinking, feeling, mood, and behavior. They may be occasional or long-lasting. They can affect your ability to relate to others and function each day" (2021). Here is a list of some types of mental disorders identified by Steven Hyman, Dan Chisholm, Ronald Kessler, Vikram Patel,and Harvey Whiteford in their article titled ***Mental Disorders*** (nd):

A. **Anxiety Disorders:** these are a group of mental health disorders that include general anxiety disorders, social phobias, specific phobias, panic disorders, obsessive compulsive disorders (OCD) and post-traumatic stress disorder (PTSD). A person suffering from this disorder has symptoms of panic, being too scared, irritated, excessive worry, waiting for bad news.

In church, they will always make small church differences as huge. They may even have bad dreams and nightmares of the people they have had misunderstanding with, and begin to accuse them of spiritually attacking them. Untreated, anxiety disorders can lead to significant confusion among church members.

B. **Bipolar Disorder:** this is a type of two extreme mood disorder. At one point a person with bipolar disorder experiences episodes of calm, collectiveness, happiness, joy, friendliness and at another point they can be very uncontrollable, violent, rude and unfriendly. A very tense church environment can trigger episodes of this mental illness. Bipolar disorder is like having two people in one.

Today they may be happy to see you and greet you joyfully in church and tomorrow they may not be in a good mood and they may behave in an uncontrollable manner.

C. **Paranoid:** this is the irrational and persistent feeling that people are "out to get you." Paranoia may be a symptom of conditions including paranoia personality disorder. Delusional (paranoia) disorder and schizophrenia.

Symptoms include; constant thoughts of being fought. A church member withparanoia always thinks that everyone in church is fighting them. They may even think they have a demon of rejection causing people not to love them. Such people are likely to have quarrels and differences with everyone regardless of which church department they join. They usually play victim all the time and can be very difficult to correct, discipline or work with.

Someone always asked me to pray for them. They claimed to be was under spiritual attacks all the time. They said the people attacking them were from the church, and most of the time they would always locked up themselves in the house, that their neighbors began to get worried. Sometimes they would have so much mood swings that they wouldn't talk to people. At other times they would just be locked up in prayer and fasting, binding spirits they supposed where after them. They believed those spirits were sent to them by the people who were fighting them. One day, they called me for prayer again, and I just thought they didn't need prayer but counseling because I noticed their problem was more of a mental problem than spiritual. I went to see them and suggested they see a therapist for her issues. That's when I found out that they had actually been treated for mental illness before. It appears they were suffering from paranoia and a delusional disorder.

I remember another lady in church who always came to me complaining about how people are fighting her. I moved her from one department to another, and it was the same story. After a great while I understood it was nothing spiritual but a mental health issue. You will find such people suffering from mental illness in church.

Understanding this will help you to be patient and compassionate with others.

D. **Delusional Disorder:** this is a mental illness where one has a permanently fixed delusion. A delusion is something that someone believes to be real regardless of contrary evidence.

There are two types of delusions. A non-bizarre delusion and bizarre delusion. A bizarre delusion is an "out of this world" delusion that someone believes. For example, believing that the sky is falling down on you is a bizarre delusion. It is impossible that the sky would fall on you, but delusional people believe and as such act like the sky is falling on them.

A non-bizarre delusion is something that someone can believe. For example, if an accountant stops work and start a big business immediately. Someone can begin to believe that he stole money from his previous company. That's a possible believable non-bizarre delusion.

In church, indeed people suffer from bizarre and non-bizarre delusions. As a single man, it's easy for one to believe you are fornicating with any lady someone finds in your house. That's a non-bizarre delusion. But it's a bizarre delusion for one to claim that you have made pregnant a woman whom you have never met physically.

I have encountered people who have bizarre delusions about me. A certain lady from a certain country apparently had a vison that I was supposed to marry her and she had three children with me in the spirit realm. That's a bizarre delusional disorder.

A story is told of a great man of God who was married with children but a certain lady was convinced that God had told her that the man was her husband and so she began to pray and fast for hundred days so that the current wife would die and she should become the new wife. That's a lady with a bizarre delusional disorder.

Most bizarre delusions are wrapped up with religious wrappings. I know a man who always saw things and heard voices of his former prophet trying to kill him. In the early stages of his hallucinations, many actually thought he was truly seeing visions of God. As the mental illness grew worse, the man would run like a mad man to the road claiming that his former prophet was trying to kill him. He was later taken to a mental institution for treatment.

Certain church members may have a delusion that some fellow church members are witches. They may even dream about them trying to bewitch them. This delusion becomes so deep in them that they begin to spread the rumors that the individual is a witch. Some family members demonize their old grandmothers and aunties to be witches.

Note that I believe witchcraft is real and some people are truly witches, but in this chapter, I am discussing mental health issues, and not spiritual issues. Some people who spread witchcraft stories in church are simply people suffering from delusional disorders. You need to have discernment for you to know the difference. The enemy uses these illnesses to further cause confusion in the church and deepen church hurt. I have had members who were accused to be witches and false rumors were created about them.

Another symptom is that a person with a bizarre delusional disorder refutes all evidence presented to them but choses to rather believe what their mind tells them. If they believe you are fake, then you are fake. If they believe they saw you entering a bar, it doesn't matter what evidence you provide, even if you showed them your passport that you were out of the country at the time, they are saying you went to the bar, they will still hold on to what they have concluded. What they believe is true to them. It's a mental illness called delusional disorder.

As I mentioned earlier, these are purely mental health issues and of course the devil and his evil spirits take advantage of them and usethese illnesses to further cause confusion and scatter people away from church.

Child of God, you might have been hurt in church by a person with a mental illness. You might have been offended in church by people suffering from various mental disorders. You stopped serving God because of someone who has a mental health case. Maybe it was even your pastor or your leader. Maybe it was even your prayer partner who hurt you while they were going through a mental illness.

The devil takes advantage of people's weaknesses and uses them against the church. Could it be that he successfully managed to get out of the church using his ancient tricks? Could it be that you are among the statistics of people who really love God but were overcome by the devil's church hurt tricks?

It's time for you to remove yourself from the devil's statistics of those he managed to get out of church service. Your place is in church. Join our Lord Jesus Christ's mission and vision *"I will build my church and the gates of hell shall not prevail against it"*(Matt 16:18). No matter how many times the enemy is fighting the church, he will not succeed because you are coming back home to fulfill your mandate in the house of the

Lord. Praise God! Don't hate church, overcome church hurt!

David said, *"A day in the house of the Lord is better than a thousand years elsewhere"*(Psalm 84:10a). He surely had his fair share of troubles but he knew that the house of the Lord was his safe place. He said again, *"I would rather be a door keeper in the house of the Lord"*(Psalm 84:10b). David's revelation of God's house is a great blessing. No wonder he was a man after God's own heart. He loved God's house so much and all he wanted to do was to build God's house.

Personality Disorders

When a person has a personality disorder, they display behaviors that you would not expect from them based on their culture and background. According to Mayo Clinic (2016), "a personality disorder is a type of mental disorder in which you have a rigid and unhealthy pattern of thinking, functioning and behaving. A person with a personality disorder has trouble perceiving and relating to situations and people. This causes significant problems and limitations in relationships, social activities, work and school."

When someone has a personality disorder, they are inflexible and unable to change their minds, patterns and behavior. You may counsel them, take them to the church council or board of deacons and elders, you may spend time talking to them, but they will not change their minds nor their behavior. Sometimes people claim church hurt when actually they have a conflict with their personality disorders.

Here are few personality disorders discussed by various Psychologists and Mental Illness experts:

1. **Narcissistic Personality Disorder:** a person with this disorder is a kind of person who is power hungry. They want to be the spotlight in everything. They are preoccupied with prestige and status. Such people are self-centered and want everything to go their way.

   When someone with this personality disorder is in church leadership, they will always fight for their ideas to be followed by everyone else, especially if they occupy high positions in church. They will be completely obsessed to control everything and want everyone to praise them for their achievements. They are great attention seekers and overly selfish.

2. **Avoidant Personality Disorder:** A person with this personality disorder does not take criticism well. Telling them where they are wrong is the end of peace in the church. They are extremely sensitive to correction and rebuke. When you rebuke or criticize such kind of a person, they go under self-isolation and withdraw from church members and church activities.

Such people suffer from low self-esteem and will feel very sad whenever confronted about their errors or mistakes. You can't call them and sit them down for accountability. They will do everything possible to avoid confrontation and criticism of their mistakes as they are too sensitive and break down easily.

3. **Borderline Personality Disorder:** This personality disorder is characterized by

unstable mood swings, makes one to be indecisive. An indecisive person is not stable in all his ways. A person suffering from this disorder is always unstable, unsure, unreliable, undecided.

People with borderline personality disorder, especially when occupying a position of leadership tend to hamper progress and bring instability in the church because of the confusion of their constant indecisive state of mind.

4. **Dependent Personality Disorder:** A person with this kind of disorder is extremely depended on others for everything. They expect to be taken care of by everyone else. You will hear them complain about how the church does not care for them adequately. They may not even be employed by the church but will always want to depend on the church.

They desire to live with rich members of the church so that they can be taken care of. They are in danger of being abused and taken advantage of if they find themselves in the wrong hands.Such a person will move from one church to another.

Depression

Depression is a mood disorder characterized by low mood, loss of interest in life, loss of interest in church programs, loss of interest in enjoyment and reduced energy. It is beyond a normal kind of feeling sad. There are different types and symptoms of depression. There are also varying levels of severity and symptoms related to depression.

Symptoms of depression can be severe sadness, irritability, lying in bed all day and night but not sleeping. Depression can lead to increased risk of suicidal thoughts or bad behaviors such as abuse of alcohol, drugs and extreme compulsive sexual activities and use of social media. Another symptom may be constantly feeling sick without knowing why. Doctors will have to carefully examine the source of pain before diagnosing depression and prescribing treatment. Constant struggles, fears, and feeling a sense of failure to measure up to other people's successes can bring exhaustion, fatigue, hopelessness, depression and even make one suicidal.

People with depression may be very difficult to work with in church, especially if they occupy strategic church positions. They may be absent for crucial services or meetings just on the basis that they were nursing feelings of depression by lying in bed and feeling sad. People who feel offended and hurt emotionally can plunge into depression.

Elijah was a prophet who felt so offended by God that he asked God to kill him. He felt God was not caring enough for him that he lived a very difficult life of being misunderstood, always hiding from his enemies, running like a fugitive. Elijah got to a point where he became so tired that he ran into the wilderness and asked God to kill him. He felt he was a failure and was not like his fathers. Elijah plunged into depression and suicidal thoughts beclouded his mind. But God reached out to him, comforted him and refreshed him and set him up to focus on finishing his mission.

"But he himself went a day's journey into the wilderness and came and sat down under a broom tree. And he prayed that he might die, and said, 'It is enough! Now, Lord, take my life, for I am no better than my fathers" (1 Kings 19:4).

Jesus as He was having His last supper with His disciples, He said by the revelation of God that one of them was going to betray Him, and His words pained and hurt every one of them. But that was not all. After supper, he took His disciples to a place called Gethsemane and asked them to sit at some point while he went to pray at a distance. Then he took with Him Peter, James and John and began to show grief, distress of mind and deep depression. He opened up to them and said that he was actually very distressed and depressed to the point of almost dying. He asked them to watch and pray for Him while He went into prayer himself. But they slept, their energies were drained by the feelings of sorrow,because of the words He had told them. Jesus prayed for hours dealing with depression because of the impending sufferings of betrayal from a close friend, the false accusations, the insults, the shame, the violent punishment and death of a common criminal that awaited Him.The thought of seeing the Father turning His back on Him because of Him becoming the sin of the world by taking all the sins of human beings on Himself on the cross ahead could be deeply depressing. The thought of darkness over fellowship that He had always enjoyed with the Father (though it would just be a temporary silence and broken fellowship) was very depressing. He was depressed to the point of almost dying. But he dealt with it through the fervent prayer of surrender to the Father's will. He prayed to the point of His sweat dropping like thick drops of blood, and God sent an angel to strengthen Him. Praise God!

*"And as they were eating, He said, 'Solemnly I say to you. one of you will betray Me!' They were exceedingly pained and distressed and deeply hurt and sorrowful and began to say to Him one after another, 'Surely it cannot be I, can it?' ... And when they had sung a hymn, they went out to the Mount of Olives... Then Jesus went to a place called Gethsemane, and He told His disciples, 'Sit down here while I go over yonder and pray. And taking with Him Peter and the two sons of Zebedee, **He began to show grief and distress of the mind and was deeply depressed**. Then He said to them, 'My soul is very sad and deeply grieved, so that I am almost dying of sorrow. Stay here and keep awake and keep watch with Me"* (Matt 26:21,22,30,36-38 Amplified).

*"And there appeared to Him an angel from heaven, strengthening Him in spirit. And **being in an agony of mind**, He prayed all the more earnestly and intently, and His sweat became like*

great clots of blood dropping down upon the ground. And when He got up from prayer, He came to the disciples and found them sleeping from grief" (Luke 22:43-45 Amplified)

Depression is very common, even among believers today. Jesus too went through severe depression. Notice that one may be depressed and those around him don't even know it. They were all having fun at supper. Although Jesus mentioned something that hurt everyone while they were eating, nobody could notice the agony and distress of mind and the deep depression Jesus was going through. They even sung a hymn together and nobody noticed it. When they got to the garden of Gethsemane, Jesus asked His disciples to wait at some place while he went to a distant place to pray, and taking Peter, James and John with Him, His closest friends, he opened up to them and confided in them about what He was going through and asked them to stand with Him in prayer while He too prayed.

Here we see some antidote to depression from Jesus' way of dealing with it. He opened up to those he could trust, asked for their help through prayer and He himself went into fervent prayer. There are so many people dying of depression and so many even committing suicide because they have not opened up to anyone. Depression is a very subtle but lethal mental illness. When you share your depression with somebody you trust, you weaken its hold on you. Seeing a therapist can help many come out of depression. Furthermore, sharing it to confidant friends that can stand with you in prayer while you also pray about it would just stripe depression and heaviness from you. Why? There is the mental side, emotional side and physical side to depression. Depression also has a spiritual dimension to it.

Some depression patients are prescribed anti-depressants. However, do not underestimate the effectiveness of counseling and the power of prayer as weapons to break the back of depression.

*"Is anyone among you suffering? Let him pray...
The effective fervent prayer of a righteous man
avails much"* (James 5:13a,16b)

The church has failed to help many people to come out depression. Most believers actually are more concerned about criticizing those going through depression as weak brethren that lack faith in God, and pointing out that those who commit suicide, even as a result of depression go straight to hell. It is very unfortunate. Very few think about helping those going through depression. When you have a depressed people in church, there is an atmosphere of heaviness.

The church society is a mixture of mentally healthy people as well as those that come with mental illnesses and disorders. We cannot pretend we just have mentally stable people in church. Most people have been hurt in church because they encountered someone with a mental disorder or a personality disorder and they did not know it. Most people's mental illness problems are not taken seriously by the church as to address them. It is important to exercise patience, empathy and compassion for people with depression.

Many people have gone through stress, grief, depression, trauma and other experiences that have had serious impact on their mental health. In most cases the church has failed to effectively help such people. Others fail to properly take care of their mental health. This has perpetuated the rise in more mental health cases in the church. In most cases the church is on the forefront criticizing the depressed to be a people lacking faith, the grieving to be people constantly seeking attention, and those committing suicide to be candidates for hell fire. Shame on us! As the church, we are the body of Christ – (hands, feet, mouth, ears, eyes, hands, and other parts of Christ). We are to listen and see and extend help to those going through things affecting their mental health.

CHAPTER 12

A Ministry to the Homosexual Community

*Do you not know that the unrighteous will not inherit the kingdom of God? Do not be deceived. Neither fornicators, nor idolaters, nor adulterers, nor homosexuals, nor sodomites, nor thieves, nor covetous, nor drunkards, nor revilers, nor extortioners will inherit the kingdom of God. And **such were some of you. But you were washed**, but **you were sanctified,** but **you were justified** in the name of the Lord Jesus and by the Spirit of our God*

(1 Corinthians 1:9-11).

One of the hot issues affecting the church today is the issue of gay rights. The church has been challenged on confronting the matters of Lesbian Gay Bisexual Transgender and Questioning rights mostly referred to as LGBTQ rights. In this chapter we shall pay attention to this particular subject and discuss how it relates to church hate. The LGBTQ community recently has grown and raised its voice. We have seen certain nations and Christian denominations endorse the LGBTQ rights. As I alluded to earlier, the church is comprised of different people with different backgrounds. Such people include the lesbians, the gay, the bisexual, the transgender and several other people with different sexual preferences or orientations.

God's stance is clear on homosexuality and we must adhere to it. *"Do not practice homosexuality, having sex with another man as with a woman. It is a detestable sin" "If a man practices homosexuality, having sex with another man as with a woman, both men have committed a detestable act. They must both be put to death, for they are guilty of a capital offense"* (Leviticus 18: 22, 20:13, NLT).

But just as we have fornicators, adulteress in church, we also have homosexuals (people who are sexually attracted to the same sex). It is clear from scripture that homosexuality is a sin, but the reality is that church folk commit this sin.

The church is therefore left with two options which are; to either reject the homosexual believers or embrace them. The church can either open its doors for them or shut them out. The church can either continue to condemn them or come up with biblical means of helping them.

We have heard of scandals of homosexual abuse among pastors, priests, fathers and church members. It is no longer shocking but a reality that we have homosexuals standing in pulpits as well as sitting in church pews. Today we see the pastors and priests blessing same sex marriages. Some people's first exposure to homosexuality was from church. They came to church and found a friend at church who was either bisexual, lesbian or gay and introduced them to this lifestyle.

I also understand that one's sexual orientation is deeply rooted in one's biological makeup. I strongly believe abnormal sexual orientation is traced from the sin or fall of man. God does instantly transform someone immediately at salvation. But on the other hand, some issues require a process in order for someone to be transformed. Certain issues in one's biological makeup and character require a process of attention, counseling and prayer. Some people go through a long process for them to experience God's total transformation after salvation. God does not hate homosexuals but hates homosexuality. The church should brace and equip itself in tackling this reality.

Ministering to Homosexuals

Instead of condemning the homosexuals and harshly judging them. The church must create a deliberate ministry to these people and point them to the saving grace of our Lord Jesus Christ. The church must look at homosexuals as candidates for salvation and not candidates for prison. The ministry of Jesus Christ to all sinners including the homosexuals is to point all of them to the cross for salvation. Homosexuals must not be treated as different kinds of sinners from other sinners. All need the love of Christ. All need the power of God to transform their lives. All need Jesus to change their ways. All need our love. We have a responsibility to share the love of Jesus to the homosexuals and trust Him for their transformation. In 1 Corinthians Paul indicates that homosexuals were among the recipients of God's salvation and were part of the Corinthian Church. The grace of our Lord Jesus invites all people (gays and lesbians inclusive) to salvation.

*Do you not know that the unrighteous will not inherit the kingdom of God? Do not be deceived. Neither fornicators, nor idolaters, nor adulterers, nor homosexuals, nor sodomites, nor thieves, nor covetous, nor drunkards, nor revilers, nor extortioners will inherit the kingdom of God. And **such were some of you. But you were washed**, but **you were sanctified,** but **you were justified** in the name of the Lord Jesus and by the Spirit of our God (1 Cor 1:9-11).*

Paul is here very candid in mentioning all the sins as the reason for attracting the wrath of God and points out that the fornicators, adulterers, homosexuals, sodomites, thieves, the covetous, drunkards, revilers and extortioners shall not inherit the Kingdom of God. But he quickly points all these sinners to the grace of God in Christ Jesus in the next verse and reminds the Corinthians that they were once among these named sinners but have been **washed, sanctified** and **justified** in the name of Jesus.

Note that in this passage the homosexuals, sodomites, gays and lesbians are among the *washed, sanctified and justified*. This passage gives enough testimony that there is hope for the homosexuals to experience the power of God for salvation and later on to experience transformation. The church must never look at homosexuals as candidates of God's wrath and condemnation, instead, it must look at them as among the recipients of His love and grace. God loves homosexuals and He wants them **washed, sanctified** and **justified** just like all other sinners. The church must look at the homosexuals as lost souls who need salvation.

We must forgo and ignore church protocols, traditions and all the customs that make us look at homosexuals with a judgmental eye. Instead, we must stretch the love of God and point them to the cross of our Lord Jesus Christ for salvation. If we don't reach out to the homosexuals with His love, we shall not manage to draw them to Jesus. We must remember that the secular movement is out there grouping the LGBTQ people into communities and making them believe that their desires are perfectly normal and okey. This has made it even more complicated to show this community the need for salvation. Without reaching out to the LGBTQs with love, we shall fail to effectively present the Gospel to them.

Somebody must not be rejected from the church just because of the homosexual fantasies and desires. The church must be a place of healing even for the homosexuals. We need to create an environment in church where homosexuals would seek help and find healing. No homosexual will be transformed through hatred. All sinners only experience genuine transformation when they encounter the love of God. When Jesus died on the cross, he took away all the condemnation and carried the wrath of God that was supposed to be ours on himself. Jesus died for the homosexuals too. Jesus saves homosexuals too. Jesus transforms homosexuals too. If Jesus has delivered you from fornication, adultery and other sins he can deliver homosexuals as well. If Jesus loves you regardless of your adultery, fornication and other sins; he loves the gays regardless of their homosexual sins as well. We all need the grace of our Lord Jesus Christ. Homosexuals are not excluded from experiencing this grace of our Lord Jesus Christ.

CHAPTER 13

STEPTS TO OVERCOME CHURCH HURT

"For whatever is born of God overcomes the world, and this is the victory that has overcome the world – our faith. Who is he who overcomes the world, but he who believes that Jesus is the Son of God?" (1 John 5:4-5)

Overcoming church hurt is honestly not easy but a possibility you have to embrace. I honestly cannot guarantee you that you will not be hurt again by someone in church. I can assure you that something will happen that will attempt to hurt you terribly.

I have grown up in church. Definitely much of my painful experiences in life have come from church. I have been kicked out of a house by a ministry I once ministered in and I didn't know where to go. I was homeless.I've been loved by church folk and deeply hated by the same people. It is always amazing how we can switch from love to hate. But I eventually learnt how to let go of all the pain with the help of the great comforter, the Holy Spirit.

Here are some of the steps you can take to experience healing from church hurt:

STEP 1

Have a Positive Attitude towards God: When we have been hurt by God's people, it affects how we see God and we developa negative attitude towards Him. Church hurt makes you start doubting if you are really loved by God.You begin to think He doesn't care enough for you;otherwise, why would He allow you to go through all that pain and hurt from His house. It's very important that you know and believe that His thoughts for you are not evil but always good. Separate church hurt from God's character of love.

STEP 2

Accept that you have been hurt and you are hurting: I know it sounds difficult but acceptance of what has happened to you is the foundation of your healing process. Stop denying the hurt you feel, stop suppressing it, stop ignoring it but face it and accept the fact that you are hurting. Denial is never the correct path to healing. Healing starts when we accept that we hurting. It is only when we accept that we are hurting that we shall be willing to follow the process of healing.

STEP 3

Find the main area in which you hurt the most: Pin point the issue that really hurts you. Identify your area of pain in order to take the right prescription. It's important to do this so that you not are just hurting over something you can't really explain. Is it something that happened to you directly or was it someone close to you whom you saw going through church hurt? Take time and write down everything you can remember.

STEP 4

Let it out before the Lord: Before you talk to anyone about your pain, talk to the One who really can help you and heal you from it all. One thing we learn from David is he always let out his feelings, pains and emotions before the Lord. We usually feel free to tell everyone about our pain except the Holy Spirit our comforter. Talk to Him first.

STEP 5

Find someone sober and mature in Christ to talk to: I advise you find a mature Christian counselor who will help you see in things in perspective. Find someone with whom you will be comfortable to share your pain and be free to breakdown in their presence. If possible, find someone within your local church, but if not, you can still seek help from someone elsewhere as long as that person ismature in Christ.Open up to that mature person and pour out your heart. A problem shared is half solved.

STEP 6

Remember you must forgive: You have to eventually come to a place where you let them go without suffering punishment for all the hurt, they caused you. I don't know how deeply they hurt you, or your family, or your ministry, but you will need to forgive them of all they have done. Let God be the one to deal with them. Forgive because Christ has also forgiven you greatly. Forgive so that you might be forgiven.

STEP 7

You may go for confrontation: Sometimes people hurt you unknowingly, they may not even be aware of the pain they caused you. But some people are too toxic to confront. Just leave them to God but forgive them. Do not confront before you forgive. If you must confront them, depending on the situation, don't confront them alone, go with a counselor or someone mature.

STEP 8

Take your mental and emotional healing: Our Lord Jesusis closer to those hurting. His anointing is to heal the broken hearted. Take advantage of the inner healing Christ has for you in abundance. Like David, stop crying and begin to encourage yourself in the Lord.

STEP 9

Restore your spiritual strength through studying the word and spending time in prayer: Studying God's word and spending time with Him in prayer will instill spiritual strength in you to deal with hurt and painful situations. The word and the presence of God have a way of restoring supernatural strength in us to live above our hurts and problems.

STEP 10

Be thankful to God and focus on seeing the best in people: This is not deflecting or ignoring the reality of hurt but it is so refreshing and restoring. When you are thankful to God in every circumstance you actually yield and get closer to Him.When you are closer to God, He also gets closer to you.This brings benefits of healing, refreshment and restoration from His presence. Begin to see the best in people beyond their negative side. This will enable you to understand them more and to also realize that they are good human beings in spite of them having a negative side. Everybody has a bad side and a good side.Above all be thankful to God for your life.

CHAPTER14

RECEIVING HEALING FROM CHURCH HURT

"But for you who fear My name, the Sun of Righteousness will rise with healing in His wings. And you will go free, leaping with joy like calves let out to pasture" (Malachi 4:2 NLT)

HOW TO RECEIVE HEALING FROM CHURCH HURT

1. Yield Yourself to the Holy Spirit for Healing

You may be a victim of church hurt and you could still be in pain or have even left church as a result of it. You can heal from that hurt and pain. Jesus, the Sun of Righteousness will rise with healing in His wings and the glorious light and warmth of His Holy Spirit will heal you, set you free and bring you back the joy of salvation and liberty.

The coming of Jesus in the earth was for our healing and comfort. His work of healing and comforting has continued after His resurrection and ascension through His Spirit. The Holy Spirit is our counselor, comforter, helper and guide. To receive your inner healing from church hurt, you will need the help, comfort, counsel and guidance of the Holy Spirit directly through personal prayer and fellowship with Him or indirectly through godly people that are Spirit filled and sensitive to Him.

*"And I will ask the Father, and **He will give you another Comforter** (Counselor, Helper, Intercessor, Advocate, Strengthener, and Standby), that He may remain with you forever – the Spirit of Truth... I will not leave you as orphans (comfortless, desolate, bereaved, forlorn, helpless); I will come back to you... **Peace I leave with you; My own peace I now give you and bequeath to you**. Not as the world gives do I give to you. Do not let your hearts to be troubled, neither let them be afraid (Stop allowing yourself to be agitated and disturbed; and do not permit yourself to be fearful and intimidated and cowardly and unsettled)"*

(John 14:16-18,27 Amplified).

Your situation is not beyond remedy. Don't allow that hurt you got from church to agitate you and to disturb you. Don't let it continue keeping you in that pain. There is a better life you can live. A life free of hurt, pain andgrudges. A life rich in health both mentally and emotionally. You cannot afford to continue living a life of pain and regret all the time. Let go of that hurt and pain; lay it upon the Lord and allow Him to heal you.

One of the works of the Spirit in you as a believer is to bring comfort to you when you are emotionally in pain or grief. Grief is a feeling of loss. Church hurt makes you lose a lot. You lose love, peace, strength, friends, fellowship, and you could even lose your mental health. Church hurt takes a lot away from you. But through the Holy Spirit, you have an opportunity to receive healing and to get restored.

Remember Jesus said that in this world we shall have trouble, distress, trials, frustration, including hurt but we must take courage, be confident and be undaunted in Him that He has overcome the world.

Church hurt is not a surprise to Jesus. That is what is in the world. You would ask why you could have been hurt right in church.But always remember that the church society is comprised of all kinds of people, including people from the world and those that may still be influenced by the devil.

"I have told you these things, so that in Me you may have perfect peace and confidence. In the world you have tribulation and trials and distress and frustration; but be of good cheer (take courage, be confident, certain, undaunted)! For I have overcome the world (I have deprived it of power to harm you and have conquered it for you)" (John 16:33 Amplified).

2. Allow Yourself To Be Vulnerable Again

Obviously, emotional hurt, including that which is associated with offenses from church has a way of causing so much pain, and making you to withdraw from those who may have caused it. It may even have made you build walls around you and gatesto make you safe from further hurt. But those walls and gates could also be keeping you bound and away from a life of freedom, love and fellowship. Withdraw also keeps you from the people God could use to bring you healing.

"A brother offended is harder to win over than a strong city, and contentions are like the bars of a castle" (Prov 18:19).

When most people get hurt by others, they get to blame themselves for allowing others to hurt them. This leads them to building defensive walls that complicate their associations and relationships. They put up defense mechanisms like being withdrawn, not being open, stopping to attend church and fellowship, stopping to socialize, being aggressive, lashing out at anybody who comes close to them, deflecting to having a busy life engrossed only into work. You could be that person that was hurt and you have now fortified yourself like that. The truth is, you may have fortified yourself from further external hurt, but you are also keeping a lot of good things and good people out of your life.

To receive healing from church hurt or even any other hurts from people, you need to make yourself vulnerable again. Open up to God and to somebody else. Give yourself a chance to experience life in church and fellowship with others. Not all people are the same, and God's character is not to be confused with the behaviors of some church folk. God wants you well and happy.

What I am asking of you is not easy but it is also not impossible. It is hard but you can do it.I am simply asking you to let go of the hurt and allow God to heal you.

3. Forgive and Let Go

Unforgiveness brings and perpetuates emotional torment and bondage while forgiveness is so liberating and restoring. Somebody said, keeping a grudge is like drinking poison and yet expecting another person to die from it. When you forgive, you actually free yourself from the hurt in your heart. Church hurt reaches deep into one's heart, and therefore, forgiveness too has to be from the heart.

"Should you not also have had compassion on your fellow servant, just as I had pity on you? And his master was angry, and delivered him to the tormentors until he should pay all that was due to him. So My heavenly Father also will do to you if each of you, from his heart, does not forgive his brother his trespasses" (Matt 18:33-35).

When you forgive, you not only do it for the one who has offended you but you actually do it for your own freedom and healing. It has been proven scientifically that some people that keep grudges for a long time end up developing arthritis (an inflammation of a joint causing disability, swelling and stiffness). Obviously, there are other causesof this condition but keeping grudges and emotional hurts is one of them.

For if you forgive other people when they sin against you, your heavenly Father will also forgive you. But if you do not forgive others their sins, your Father will not forgive your sins (Matthew 6:14-15, NIV)

Be kind and compassionate to one another, forgiving each other, just as in Christ God forgave you (Ephesians 4:32,NIV)

The two verses indicate to us the commandment to forgive. You must forgive so that you can be forgiven. Secondly, you must forgive because you have been forgiven. Before Christ died, we had to forgive in order for the father to forgive us. After the death of Christ on the cross, you have to forgive because you are forgiven.

4. Pray for those Who have Hurt You

Coupled with forgiving of those who may have hurt you is offering prayer for them. This is so liberating and restoring. You would think, vengeance could be the solution but no, forgiveness and prayer for them is.

Jesus taught us to love our enemies, bless those who curse us, be kind to those who hate us and pray for those who abuse us and persecute us. He insisted that this was the mark of being a true child of God.

"You have heard that it was said, 'You shall love your neighbor and hate your enemy,' but I say, love your enemies, bless those who curse you, do good to those who hate you, and pray for those who spitefully use you and persecute you, that you may be sons of your Father in heaven; for He makes His sun to rise on the evil and on the good, and sends rain on the just and on the unjust" (Matt 5:43-45).

God doesn't forgive us or bless us because we deserve it. Forgiveness is undeserved unearned favor. Forgiveness is simply having mercy and giving grace to somebody who has done you wrong and therefore doesn't even deserve it. Forgiveness is not selective. God doesn't choose whom he gives rain and cause His sun to shine on, but He gives to everybody without segregating.

You cannot be a Christian and you have this language:"I will not forgive that one for what she did to me!" No! That should not be in the vocabulary of a Christian. For you as a Christian, forgiveness is one of the values and beliefs in your faith. Praying for your haters and those that abuse and hurt you is also one of the core values and beliefs of your faith. There is healing in forgiving and praying for those who hurt you.

"Confess your sins to each other and pray for each other so that you may be healed. The earnest prayer of a righteous person has great power and produces results" (James 5:16 NLT)

Job went through a difficult time of his life. His ten children got killed by a storm in one day, his all wealth got stolen, he lost his physical health and his own wife lost respect for him. His family members abandoned him and his friends blamed him for what he was going through. They said he had sinned and needed to repent in order to experience restoration. Their words lacked grace and hurt deep into his heart. But Job forgave them. God rebuked his friends and instructed them to go and receive prayer from Job. When Job forgave them and prayed for them, God healed him and restored him and blessed his latter days more than the beginning.

"And the Lord restored Job's losses when he prayed for his friends. Indeed, the Lord gave Job twice as much as he had before... Now the Lord blessed the latter days of Job more than his beginning..." (Job 42:10-12).

You too can heal from that hurt you got from church. Forgive those who hurt you and pray for them for your own sake. Keeping grudges is keeping the blessing away and far from yourself. Forgive, let go, and pray for those who hurt you. Your miracle of healing and other breakthroughs is in your ability to forgive and pray for those who have hurt you.

5. Accept God's Love and Comfort

No matter your pain and hurt, God wants to reach out to you with His love, compassion and comfort. Mostly, when you are hurt by other people, you may feel unloved, abandoned and neglected even by God. However, no matter how you feel, God is still with you, He loves you, He cares for you and He has promised that He will never leave you nor abandon you. You will need to come to terms with God's love and providence. God is not like those who hurt you. God is not to be confused with how you feel. God is who He says He is.

*"Praise be to the God and Father of our Lord Jesus Christ, the Father of **compassion** and the God of all **comfort**, who comforts us in all our troubles, so that we can comfort those in any trouble with the comfort we ourselves receive from God"* (2 Cor 1:3-4 NIV).

You will need to believe and accept God's love and comfort. Believing and accepting God's love and comfort will heal you and empower you to equally be able to share with other hurting people the same love and comfort that you have received and experienced. Healing from church hurt by receiving God's love and comfort will empower you to serve God again. ***You can serve God again.***

6. There is no Condemnation for those who are in Christ Jesus

The Bible declares that *"There is therefore now no condemnation for them who are in Christ"* (Rom 8: 1). This verse is like a lie to many believers in day-to-day Christianity. Some people behave as though this scripture cannot be applied by fellow believers. Stronger believers feel it's a verse for those who want to continue living a sinful lifestyle. Those still struggling with the lusts of the flesh hold on to this verse as they find comfort in its reality.

The gift of no condemnation is one of the best Christ has given those who trust His finished work on the cross. I came to learn that I should not expect people to give me the same gift. The free gift of no condemnation only comes from Christ and if you are lucky, you might find a few people in church who may treat you like Christ.

Most of us expect to be treated without condemnation or judgment by our fellow church mate but the opposite is true. My friend, this gift of no condemnation can only come from Christ Jesus because of His great sacrifice for you on the cross. Don't expect it from anyone else. The prodigal son returned home and the father gave him the gift of no condemnation but the big brother did not. This reality is true in the church today. God will always forgive you and accept you back into fellowship with Him but the church will not easily accept you back after your failure. Always remember that as a believer in Christ, you are not condemned and you will never be condemned by the one who really matters, God.

CHAPTER 15

YOU CAN SERVE GOD AGAIN

"You intended to harm me, but God intended it for good to accomplish what is now being done, the saving of many lives" (Gen 50:20 NIV)

You Can Be Like Joseph, You Can Be Like Jesus

When you are going through church hurt, it's easy to hate the people our brothers and sisters in Christ. We tend to be vengeful towards them. However, God's intention is for usto forgive them and to actually treat them different from the treatment they gave us. If you suffered rejection from them,forgive them, embrace them and become a blessing in their lives. Such was Joseph's response towards his envious brothers'hate, envy, betrayal, rejection and ill-treatment.

Joseph had dreams to become a prominent leader. He dreamed his eleven brothers' sheaves bowing down to hissheaf. He again dreamed eleven stars and the sun and the moon bowing down to him, and he told them to his brothers. However, that did not sit well with them. The interpretation was that he would rise to prominence as a great leader above them. However, that did not mean that he would rise to greatness and his brothers would diminish to obscurity. Nonetheless, that is how the brothers interpreted it.

Joseph was Jacob's favorite son, and the brothers hated him for that. The dreams he told them just made them to hate him the more and they became envious of him. One day when he went to check on them in the field, they plotted to kill him, but when they saw a band of merchants going down to Egypt, they decided to sell him to them for 20 pieces of silver (This is so familiar). Jesus too was sold for 30 pieces of silver by his friend Judas. It was hurtful and an act of betrayal). The Ishmaelite merchants bought him and also sold him in Egypt at the slave market.

The story of Joseph speaks of a man who rose to prominence and forgave his brothers. He treated them well, settled them in the best of lands in Egypt and even gave opportunity to five of them to have an interview with King Pharaoh for jobs and land. This was despite them having hated, envied, betrayed and rejected him some 22 years before. They had really hurt him but he forgave them and embraced them. Overtime Joseph had been comforted and healed by God from the hurt and he was able to recognize the purpose of God in the pain he had gone through. He was able to use the hurt as an opportunity to serve God again by saving the same brothers and their families from the most dare famine at the time.

"Then he broke down and wept. He wept so loudly the Egyptians could hear him, and word of it quickly carried to Pharaoh's palace. 'I am Joseph,' he said to his brothers. 'Is my father still alive?' But his brothers were speechless. They were stunned to realize that Joseph was standing in front of them. 'Please come closer,' He said to them. So they came closer. And he said again, 'I am Joseph, your brother, whom you sold into

slavery in Egypt. But don't be upset, and don't be angry with yourselves for selling me to this place. It was God who sent me here ahead of you to preserve your lives. This famine that has ravaged the land for two years will last five more years, and there will be neither plowing nor harvesting. God has sent me ahead of you to keep you and your families alive and to preserve many survivors. So it was God who sent me here, not you! And He is the one who made me an adviser to pharaoh – the manager of his entire palace and the governor of all Egypt" (Gen 45:2-8 NLT)

Notice the emotions and the words from Joseph, ***"I am Joseph… Please come closer, I am Joseph, your brother…"*** He had forgiven them, and he had been longing for them despite having suffered hurt under their hands 22 years before. He still called them his brothers. Remember when they had thrown him into the pit and how he had wept, cried and pleaded with them. Now the rejected one is pleading with them again, and this time it was a plea of forgiveness, and a longing to embrace them and to be closer to them. He said to them with tears in his eyes, ***"I am Joseph, your brother. Please come close to me…"*** I am your brother. Yes, you may have hated me, been envious of me, rejected me, betrayed me and sold me but I am still your brother, come closer to me.

Joseph went further to bring his father Jacob and the whole of his family into Egypt where he nourished them and gave them the best of lands. Having been so close to King Pharaohthat he knew his thoughts and inquisitiveness, he gave five of his brothers an opportunity to interact with him. He knew Pharaoh would ask them about their occupation (profession). Joseph knew what he was doing. He prepared his brothers for the interview and oriented them on how they were to answer Pharaoh's questions if they are to get jobs and the best of lands.

"Then he said, "When Pharaoh calls for you and asks about your occupation, you must tell him, 'We, your servants, have raised livestock all our lives, as our ancestors have always done.' When you tell him this, he will let you live here in the region of Goshen, for the Egyptians despise shepherds" (Gen 46:33-34 NLT).

"Joseph took five of his brothers and presented them to Pharaoh. And Pharaoh asked the brothers, 'What is your occupation?' They replied, 'We, your servants, are shepherds, just like our

ancestors. We have come to live here in Egypt for a while, for there is no pasture for our flocks in Canaan. The famine is very severe there. So please, we request permission to live in the region of Goshen.' **Then Pharaoh said to Joseph, 'Now that your father and brothers have joined you here,choose any place in the entire land of Egypt for them to live. Give them the best land of Egypt. Let them live in the region of Goshen. And if any of them have special skills, put them in charge of my livestock too"** (Gen 47:2-6 NLT).

Joseph rather did good to his brothers that had doneevil to him. He overcame evil with good. He reciprocated their hurt with forgiveness, love and kindness.

Joseph recognized God's purpose even in the hurtful things he had gone through. He recognized God used his brothers' hurt on him to send him to Egypt to fulfil the dreams he had given him.He recognized that in the brothers' act of **selling** him into slavery, God was **sending**him into his destiny. He would later reassure them of his forgiveness and his commitment to remain kind to them after the death of their father Jacob.They thought he would change his mind and revenge the hurt they had done to him now that their father was dead.

When Joseph heard their words, he wept and cried and reassured them of his forgiveness.

"So they sent this message to Joseph, 'Before our father died, he instructed us to say to you, 'Please forgive your brothers for the great wrong they did to you – for their sin in treating you so cruelly.' So we, the servants of the God of your father, beg you to forgive our sin.' When Joseph received the message, he broke down and wept. Then his brothers came and threw themselves down before Joseph. 'Look, we are your slaves,' they said. But Joseph replied, 'Don't be afraid of me. Am I God, that I can punish you? You intended to harm me, but God intended it all for good. He brought me to this position so I could save the lives of many people. No, don't be afraid. I will continue to take care of you and your children. So he reassured them by speaking kindly to them" (Gen 50:16-21 NLT)

The story of Joseph is that of so much emotion but it is also a narrative that depicts and reveals to us how we ought to forgive and treat those that may have hurt us, including those who may have hurt us in church. When people have hurt you, forgive them and treat them opposite to the hurtful treatment they gave you. That act is how you can heal from your hurt and serve God again. You too can be like Joseph who forgave his brothers that had hurt him. Joseph saved the lives of his brothers that had hurt him and that of their families from the famine and did so much good to them. You can do exactly the same to those who have hurt you. Our Lord Jesus forgave Judas and those who crucified him. You too can be like Jesus and forgive those who have betrayed, rejected and hurt you. ***You can serve God again.***

"Jesus said, 'Father, forgive them, for they don't know what they are doing…" (Luke 23:34 NLT)

You can serve God again, and you should know and remember that there are blessings of serving God again. Here are some of the blessings of serving again:

1 **It is not in vain; you will be rewarded for it:** Serving God again is eternally rewarding. When you serve God in love and faithfulness, He will reward you. For everything you do in serving God's purpose, He will reward you.

    "Therefore, my beloved brethren, be steadfast, immovable, always abounding in the work of the Lord,

knowing that your labor is not in vain in the Lord" (1 Cor 15:28)

2 God will not forget you work and labor of love: Serving God again in love even after you have been hurt in church is rewarding. God will remember you forevery work and labor you do out of love despite the hurt you may have gone through, especially when the labor and ministry of love you give is towards those who actually hurt you.

> *"For God is not unjust to forget your work and labor of love which you have shown towards His name, in that you have ministered to the saints, and do minister"* (Hebrews 6:10)

> *"Remember me my God, for good, according to all that I have done for this people"* (Nehemiah 5:19)

3 God will honor you: Serving God again will move God to honor you. Serving is honorable and indeed God honors those that serve Him. Serving God is proof of your discipleship to Jesus. Return to serving God and see God honor you in ways you cannot imagine.

> *"If anyone serves Me, let him follow Me; and where I am, there My servant will be also. If anyone serves Me, him My Father will honor"* (John 12:26)

4 **God will bless you:** There are blessings in serving God. We don't serve God so that He can bless us, but when we serve Him, He does bless us.

> *"Therefore, they are before the throne of God, and serve Him day and night in His temple. And He who sits on the throne will dwell among them. They shall neither hunger anymore nor thirst anymore; the sun shall not strike them, nor any heat; for the Lamb who is in the midst of the throne will shepherd them and lead them to living fountains of waters. And God will wipe away their tears from their eyes"* (Rev 7:15-17).

"So you shall serve the Lord your God, and He will bless your bread and your water. And I will take away sickness away from the midst of you. No one shall suffer miscarriage or be barren in your land; I will fulfill the number of your days" (Ex 23:25-26)

5 **The difference shall be clear:** God will spare you and put a distinction between you and those who do not serve him. As much as you are set apart to serve God, God will ensure you are spared from any calamity and from Judgment, and He will actually put a distinction between you and those that don't serve Him. You are special.

"They shall be mine, says the Lord of hosts, on the day that I make them My jewels. And I will spare them as a man spares his own son who serves him. Then you shall again discern between the righteous and the wicked. Between one who serves God and one who does not serve Him" (Mal 3:17-18)

6 You will be closer to God: Serving God again will enable close proximity to God. When you serve God, you enjoy the blessing of His presence.

> *"Blessed is the man You choose, and cause to approach You, that he may dwell in Your courts. We shall be satisfied with the goodness of Your house, of Your holy temple"* (Psalm 65:4)

7 You will receive God's heritage: Serving God empowers you with God's heritage. As you get to serve God again you will receive God's heritage.Part of that heritage is having God's vindication and defense over your life against the enemy's accusations.

> *"But in that coming day no weapon turned against you will succeed. You will silence every voice raised up to accuse you. These benefits are enjoyed by the servants of the Lord; and their vindication will come from Me. I, the Lord, have spoken"* (Isaiah 54:17 NLT)

8 You will prosper in everything you do: As you serve God, He prospers you. we don't serve God with intent to prosper but we serve God because we love Him and He has commanded us to serve Him. God prospers us for our love, loyalty and obedience to Him. He is committed to prosper those who obey and serve Him.

> *"Let them shout for joy and be glad that favor my righteous cause; and let them say continually, Let the Lord be magnified, who has pleasure in the prosperity of His servant"* (Psalm 35:27)

> *"If they obey and serve Him, they shall spend their days in prosperity, and their years in pleasure"* (Job 36:11)

9 God will rebuke your enemies and they will neither touch nor harm you: Serving God moves God to protect you from being oppressed by your enemies. Servants of God have God's protection on their lives.

The whole nation of Israel was regarded by God as His anointed servants and He rebuked their enemies from doing them any harm.

> *"When they went from one nation to another, from one kingdom to another people, He permitted no one to do them wrong; yes, He rebuked kings for their sakes, saying, 'Do not touch My anointed ones and do My prophets no harm"* (Psalm 105:13-15)

10 God will turn the evil meant against you for good, to bless many people, including the very people who meant evil for you: God has a way of humbling the hurtful and elevating the hurting. God has a way of healing the hurting and empowering them to become a blessing to many people, including the very people that may have hurt them. God has an amazing way of turning and making the hurting into becoming a comforter.

> *"Joseph said to them, 'Do not be afraid, for am I in the place of God?*

But as for you, you meant evil against me; but God meant it for good, in order to bring about as it is this day, to save many people alive. Now therefore, do not be afraid; I will provide for you and your little ones.' And he comforted them and spoke kindly to them"
(Gen 50:18-21)

It's never too late. You can heal and serve God again. God is actually waiting for you to make that decision to begin serving him again. Take a step forward away from that hurt and see how God will amazingly begin to use you, even as a comforter to the hurting and the guilty. You now have a big heart to embrace almost everybody you come in contact with. You now have warm hands to show kindness to those that are in pain and are suffering. Be the bigger person! Be the better person! Be the comforter to the hurting, especially those that are suffering from church hurt. Blessed be God Almighty!

Conclusion

We have delved so deeply into this most uncommon but restorative subject, **Overcoming**

Church Hurt. Nearly all of us may have experienced some kind of hurt from church, and some of us may have even lost faith in God, in the church, and even in one another, that we ended up leaving church for the world. I am certainly confident that by now, having read this book, you have received some understanding associated with church hurt, how you can overcome it, and have come to the point of walking through the process of healing from it so that you can consequently begin serving God again. I know there are many things that hurt us. I have touched a few issues and I know there is more out there. Maybe I didn't specifically mention your exact church hurt, I also know it is not going to be easy but you can trust God to heal you from that church hurt and you can serve God again. It's not too late.

Don't give up on God, Don't give up on yourself. Don't give up on Christ's bride, Don't give upon the church, Get healing from church hurt.

You must Overcome Church Hurt! You can serve God again!

References

Bible Verse. Com. 2020. ***The Hellenists, who were they?*** Available @ https://www.bibleversestudy.com/acts/acts6-hellenists.htm (accessed on 26th May, 2022).

Hyman S, etl. Nd. ***Mental Disorders.*** Available @https://dcp-3.org (accessed on 26th May, 2022).

Mayo Clinic. 2016. ***Personality Disorders.*** Available @https://www.mayoclinic.org/diseases-conditions/personality-disorders/symptoms-causes/syc-20354463 (accessed on 26th May, 2022).

Mayo Clinic. 2021. ***Mental Illness.*** Available @ https://www.mayoclinic.org/diseases-conditions/mental-illness/symptoms-causes/syc-20374968 (accessed on 26th May, 2022).

Medline Plus. 2020. ***Mental Disorders.*** Available @ https://medlineplus.gov/mentaldisorders.html (accessed on 26th May, 2022)

Parekh, R. 2018. ***What is Mental Illness?****American Psychiatric Association. Available @ https://psychiatry.org/patients-families/what-is-mental-illness*(accessed on 26th May, 2022).